T0193434

Some other books by the Author.

i. Islamic Civilization: History, Contributions, Influence; 2006
ii. Medieval Islamic Economic Thought; 2003

LOST LIFE RECOVERED:
AN ODYSSEY

A MEMOIR

DR. S.M. GHAZANFAR

authorHOUSE®

AuthorHouse™
1663 Liberty Drive
Bloomington, IN 47403
www.authorhouse.com
Phone: 1 (800) 839-8640

Published by AuthorHouse 06/20/2019

ISBN: 978-1-7283-1332-0 (sc)
ISBN: 978-1-7283-1331-3 (e)

Print information available on the last page.

This book is printed on acid-free paper.

CONTENTS

Prologue 1

Chapter I   The Beginning: Early Traumas 3
Chapter II   Migration, My Foster Homes, My Growth 25
Chapter III   My Schools, My Friends 42
Chapter IV   Post-High School, Lahore And Back 50
Chapter V   Transition: Job Changes, Life Changes 65
Chapter VI   1958: The American Dream 79
Chapter VII   Survival Struggles, Graduation: 1958-62 93
Chapter VIII   My Anchors; My Travels 112
Chapter IX   Graduate Studies... 124
Chapter X   1965: Pakistan Visit And Marriage 131
Chapter XI   Confronting The Monster; Our Marriage......143
Chapter XII   Return To The USA; Unforeseen Hurdles ... 152
Chapter XIII   Our Children, My Job, Pakistan Visits 168
Chapter XIV   My Career, My Community 179
Chapter XV   Sentimental Journey To My Roots, Part I 185
Chapter XVI   Sentimental Journey To My Roots, Part II.... 206

Epilogue... 213
Appendix 215

**TO MY LATE FATHER
WHO GAVE ME SO MUCH IN SO LITTLE TIME**

AND

**TO THE ANCHORS OF MY LIFE:
MY WIFE, MY CHILDREN, MY FRIENDS
AND NUMEROUS WELL-WISHERS**

Memory can always be as much of a burden as it could sometimes be a blessing. While memory is never perfect, yet I have done my best to accurately portray the world in which I grew up and survived—and which also shaped me as a human-being.

PROLOGUE

This is the story of a prodigal son, whose father, having four daughters, prayed and won the demographic lottery: the son was born in April 1937. When the son not even four years old, the father, about 38 years old, mysteriously died. That's when the orphaned son's survival struggles—his odyssey—began.

Soon after, a neighborhood man becomes the step-father. He was a narcissist brute, abusive to the entire family, and exercised absolute power; the son suffered, observed and absorbed. At times, he would tie the son's hands, hang him to the upper ledge of a door, and beat him mercilessly, often the son afraid of being killed.

After India was partitioned in 1947, the family migrated to Lahore, Pakistan. Soon after, the son, now 10-years old, was abandoned by the step-father. Survival struggles intensify. The helpless mother found 'foster-homes' for the son and their patronage enabled him to complete high-school at age 14. By this time, the son discovered from his uncles that the step-father was the murderer of his father.

Now living in Karachi, the prodigal son learns some basic office skills, and despite being under 15, he finds a job as a low-level clerk-typist. From his meager income, he now must also support the step-father, or else, mother would be abused. The son lived the lie: despising the step-father, yet obedient and respectful. The struggle continues. Yet, father's memory always inspired the son to overcome the odds.

In the next few years, he moves to higher-paying jobs, last being with the U.S. AID office. He financed the younger sister's marriage. Then higher-education becomes his priority. Despite his 10-grade education, he managed to get admission, as a freshman, at Washington State University, Pullman. With one-way air-ticket and about a $100 cash, he lands at New York airport in September 1958. After 4-days of bus travel, he reaches Pullman. Soon, he starts part-time campus jobs—janitor, dishwasher, animal-pen cleaner, etc., and summer jobs in fruit-orchards and lumber-mill. But he must continue to send some money to step-father's household. The struggle continues.

Having graduated with honors, graduate study was the next goal. He earned the master's in 1964. While pursuing the doctorate, he went to Pakistan in 1965. He confronted the step-father and dislodged the lie he had lived all his life. Also, he found his lovely bride and got married. Upon return to the U.S., he completed the doctorate in 1968 and took a faculty position at the University of Idaho, Moscow. The family moved there and raised three wonderful children. After a successful academic career, with numerous awards and honors and global reputation for his research publications, he retired in 2002, though continued part-time teaching till 2008. The couple now lives, near daughter's family, in Atlanta, Ga. Lost life recovered; American dream fulfilled.

In February 2000, he took a sentimental journey to his birth-place in India. He sought comfort from the agonizing memories associated with his birth-house.

Chapter I

THE BEGINNING:
EARLY TRAUMAS

"A rather touching episode. September 4, 1977, Sunday evening: Asif and I are talking about things and then Asif started asking questions about his late grandfather. Daddy explained that he had died long ago. Asif asked why and how. I could see he was beginning to hurt. Then he said, 'I want my grandfather,' and started crying. I could not control myself, either. I picked him up, hugged and kissed him, and consoled him, though I myself was in great pain. All of this was in the den of the house. Then I carried him upstairs. I lied down with him; Mommy was there too. All three of us became rather upset emotionally. My tears were difficult to control, and so were Asif's. Finally, he calmed down and went to sleep in my arms. All of this was most painful."

———This quotation, taken from our son, Asif's Baby-Book, originally written by me on September 22, 1977.

This quote provides a clue to what my life has been all about—abandoned, forlorn, lonely, often traumatized, always challenging. Here I was being challenged by my

5-yars old son's yearning for his deceased grandfather. That yearning has also been part of my entire life. Indeed, this is an account of traumas, deprivation and desperation, struggle and survival, in the hope of combining tenderness and savage honesty. And faced with endless adversities and almost insurmountable odds, caught between hope and despair, I always wondered which would win out. And, then, I would escape from early life of profound humiliations, from the violence and my emotional prison. It is as though my early experiences had indelibly punctured my inner life with a thousand sharp cuts. How would I be resilient enough to survive?

Yet, as I matured a bit, I was quite driven and keen to pursue some yet unknown dreams of my own—to want to go beyond the ordinary, whatever that may be. Decades later, my younger son, Kashif, captured my determination to pursue my dreams. Perhaps he gleaned some words from our conversations and wrote these words on his room-wall: "There were times when there was only one meal a day. But when you are driven, you don't mind."

My father died, quite mysteriously, at a young age, perhaps in his late 30s, on Tuesday, March 18, 1941, in a small town called Phillaur, East Punjab, British India, where we lived at the time and which is my birthplace. He was a teacher at the local high school. I was almost 4 years old and this was the first traumatic shock of my young life. Along with three sisters (a fourth had died earlier), we were now orphans and our mother a widow. I faintly remember my crying while standing near the lower left leg of the bed upon which laid the body of my father, with a wrap tied around his head and chin, apparently to block the fluids from his mouth. Faint as my recollection is, I remember absorbing that shock of my infancy, so deeply embedded in my psyche.

In fact, over the years, it seems to have become ever so vivid, so much so that it bursts open just in a flash. And the thought of my late father overwhelms me. And now, on that day in September 1977, my dearest son, was yearning for his grandfather. And painfully I wondered: How could I bring him back for my son —and for myself!

1.   My Parents, My Traumas

And my father's death, though mentioned to be a 'natural' tragedy at the time, turned out to be the single most brutal mystery for my curious mind. At the time the story was that he died a natural death, suffered from cholera. While always a bit apprehensive during my early years, I usually mentioned 'cholera' as the cause of his death when anyone inquired. It was much later that I discovered that my dearest father was murdered by a beast of a creature in the neighborhood, well-acquainted with the family, who was to later become our "step-father." As I matured, while the mystery was gradually clarified for my soul, I also learned from other elders and deduced from my assimilation of knowledge of the relevant circumstances that, indeed, the murder of my father was a joint venture. One of the accomplices was the family doctor (the only one in the small town) who provided the lethal dose; but there was more. My father had been poisoned to death was the conclusion of those in the immediate neighborhood, including the monster's own father and relatives as well as my father's relatives.

My maternal uncle, a well-educated gentleman who was very close to his younger sister (my mother), kept written record of all the relevant events and facts. And, he would gently share much of this history with me during my earlier years as I was growing up. He was closely involved in managing the tragedy and its consequences; and he was deeply concerned about the well-being of his widowed sister (our mother) and her children. Much later, I had access to this diary and found corroboration of the facts recorded at the time by my late uncle. Further, the tragedy of the murder was confirmed by some surviving acquaintances (who lived in the neighborhood) whom I met during my sentimental journey to my birthplace in February 2000. At that time, I also learned that there were hammer-blows to my father's head to ensure his quick demise; and thus, the flow of bloody fluids from his mouth.

Burial of my father's body took place rather promptly, before my father's close relatives arrived from Jullundhar, a city 35-miles away. Apparently, the entire neighborhood—and beyond—knew what had happened and who the murderer was. The latter's father was most critical and was rumored to have died of the shock. Suspicious as they were, my father's relatives, especially his younger brother, wanted the body exhumed and pursue criminal investigation. Quite aware of her husband's motives, the murderer's jealous wife was also convinced of her husband's crime and wanted the body exhumed. Among the few who opposed exhumation were the murderer's sisters and some other relatives. However, under pressure from elders in the neighborhood, but specially through the intervention of my mother's brother (my uncle), the matter was hushed up—his key reason being, as noted in his diary, that he did not want the matter to become scandalous and defamatory to the family. Later, I learned from my uncle that he also provided some monetary incentives to my paternal uncle (my father's younger brother) so he won't insist on exhumation of the body.

As I have learnt from records kept by my maternal uncle, my mother and father were married in 1924 or so.

Consistent with the cultural traditions, it was an arranged marriage, same as the marriages of other two sisters. And, as I have learnt, my parents did not get along well at all. There was often tension and conflict between the two. That husband–wife alienation was apparently the background for the tragedies and traumas that my siblings and I later encountered. My father was known to be a simple man, rather casual about his mannerism. Fairly well–educated, he was a school teacher. Perhaps during the late 1920s, the family moved to a small town, Phillaur, part of the District Jullundhar, East Punjab (now India), where he was a teacher at the local high school. The family lived in a rented a house, owned by the family of the individual who eventually was the source of our calamities. That's where my sisters and I were born: the eldest, born in 1926, another born around 1928 or so, had become blind and deaf from some sickness and died at about age 8; third, born around 1930, died in infancy; and fourth, born around 1931, died (about July 1947, just before India's partition) of tuberculosis at age 16. As I found in family records, I was born on April 1, 1937; and then another sister, was born about 1939 or so; she passed away in February 2017.

Having four daughters already, my father yearned for a son, a deeply–embedded cultural wish. A son not only is viewed as the "social security" for parents as they age, but also one who would carry the family name into future generations. Birth of a son is viewed as the "jackpot" in the demographic lottery. Similar preference for sons prevails in almost all societies, though intensity of preference may vary. My father would go to various religious seers and shrines, pray to God for giving him a son, give charity and beseech others to pray for a son on his behalf. God Almighty heard his prayers, and he got his "jackpot;" and I was born in 1937.

But, alas, he did not live to nurture and love his son beyond the first few years. I am told he would always carry me around on his shoulders, even when I could walk. If anyone told him to let me walk, he would answer, "I am my son's horse; and a rider does not come off his horse!"

But I didn't know my father at all; I have no memory. I do not know what he looked like; I have not been able to find his picture anywhere, despite intense efforts. I never had that inner joy of calling anyone 'Dad" (or, 'Abba-ji' in the mother-tongue), except perhaps when I was a little lad. I have always yearned for the fatherly love I never received—and this yearning will linger till the day I die. His absence deprived me of my natural right of having his fatherly love and care as I was growing up. The gap left me an almost emotional cripple throughout my life, especially when I know his demise was not natural but a murder. His memory has been the single most prominent inspiration throughout my life; he gave me so much in so little time.

And at the autumn stage of my life presently, I feel absolutely convinced that this gap and the memory of my late father indeed miraculously saved me from a possibly wasted, even a criminal life, for I often felt filled with rage and about to explode. Throughout, he was my guiding light, my guardian angel. At every step and every move of my life, I always thought in terms of what he would expect of his son if he had been alive. Am I living up to his expectations? And what little I accomplished in my life, I would want him to know—perhaps he does! I have cried so often, as I do this moment, despite my aging life—just thinking of him and remembering him; there is no closure. How he would have relished some of his son's modest successes in life, how he would have liked to see his son's family and grandchildren, and great-grandchildren, etc. And, also, how my own children's childhood would have been fulfilled by their grandfather's loving presence! I know I have always felt as though he has been watching me and guiding me and judging me as to what I do in my life, what my family and children are all about, etc. And that spiritual presence of my late father has been an enormous blessing and inspiration for me, without which I probably would have been a wasted life. Oh, he wanted a son so badly! And I was the only one. And the gap has always been so painful.

And a bit more on the circumstances that led to my father's murder. Always a secret, perhaps an open secret. Obviously, the arranged marriages of my mother and her younger sister were not happy marriages, to say the least. The younger sister's unhappy marriage also resulted in considerable chaos for the family; they lived in Jullundhur, about 35 miles north of Phillaur. She had an odd alliance, aided by the fact that her husband was located, or chose to locate, several hundred miles away because of his job. The maturing children turned a blind eye to the amorous union; the individual lived in the same house. But that's another story.

The sisters shared each other's marital agonies. During an intimate conversation, decades later, my elderly cousin, my aunt's son, shared his own aches and pains; he and his siblings had helplessly seen it all, as they were growing up. As for my mother, apparently she filled her marital 'alienation-gap' by being enticed by the neighbor who had become a family friend, a frequent, visitor, and later, our "step-father"

And then the stage was set for more traumas for my life and the lives of my dearest sisters. Indeed, our late mother (passed away 1993) also suffered terribly throughout the rest of her life. In retrospect, I can honestly say, while God Almighty controls human destiny, sometimes humans bring calamities upon themselves by the choices they make of their free will; ours seems to have been that kind of a life. Yet for this soul, perhaps it worked out for the best. As I often say, my father's death gave me life.

2. "Step-father," The Monster In Our Lives

Exactly four months and fifteen days after my father's death (March 18, 1941). the second most cataclysmic event happened. My mother secretly re-married an individual, the murderer of my father. He was known to my father and the family for quite some time: he lived in the neighborhood, and had another wife, with four children. Whether this event was facilitated by any prior mutuality of interest, or forced upon my mother due to the marital discord and disharmony between my parents, or whatever other circumstances— God only knows best. The fact remains, however, that the marriage happened quite discreetly, without the knowledge of even my mother's brothers, especially the brother who cared for her so much and had assured the widowed sister that he would take care of her future well-being and that of the orphaned children. And, at the time, whenever this brother inquired about the connection with that man, my mother would simply say that he was just a "sympathetic" neighbor. From all the evidence available, the brother knew that this man was responsible for the murder of his brother-in-law, i.e., my father. The brother was vehemently against any connection with that character.

Indeed, the presence of this "step-father" set the stage for absolute misery and hardships for the entire family during the succeeding several decades. God Almighty's unbounded mercy was the only solace for this emotionally-scarred soul. As I was growing up, there was enormous comfort and affection from some good friends and their families, as well as the noble advice and guidance of a key relative—my maternal uncle, the caring elder brother of my mother. This gentleman wisely and with foresight maneuvered to take possession of some of my father's financial assets and my mother's jewelry, for he thought–so correctly–that these meager assets would be needed by the children in their future; obviously, he had no trust in the character of the new man in my mother's life, nor in her own judgement and foresight. This noble man maintained a record of all events, including the monetary-equivalent of these assets which he later utilized in the best interests of the orphaned children. My father also owned some rental property, which was part of my inheritance as being the only son. However, I had no control over the rental income; that would have been impossible even if I were an adult. The "step-father" collected the proceeds for years. And soon after the partition of India, he managed to acquire possession of the real property as well; I inherited nothing whatever.

Another individual who at the time was about the closest confidant of my mother in all that had transpired was her younger sister, who lived in Jullundhur. She had her own blemishes which the brothers despised. Apparently, some shared dark secrets of their own–as well as my mother's extreme naiveté—brought the two sisters closer. My mother was always a rather gullible woman, easily persuaded one way or the other. Any advice from her brother hardly made sense to her; and she often pretended to be paying attention to her brother's suggestions, but hardly ever did. On the other hand, the younger sister usually prevailed and my mother listened to her.

While others suspected my mother's new alliance, her sister was about the only one who knew of my mother's re-marriage when it happened. The brothers came to know of the event months later when the new husband's first wife and her relatives started spreading 'rumors,' which also caught up with the brothers. In addition, my surviving two elder sisters (about 15 and 10 years old at the time) knew as this connection evolved; in fact, my mother would often have the elder sister write rather misleading letters (preserved in his diary) to her brother, in an attempt to cover up what had been transpiring and to still seek his compassion and assistance. And, suddenly, she claimed the "sympathetic neighbor" had deceived her into signing a document that turned out to be a marriage certificate. And now she was helpless and must accept the reality of marriage; and she must accept her fate.

Regretfully, I must say, it was a charade—one that broke open later when the event was irreversible. The brother rejected his sister's explanation; and throughout my life, I always observed him as a deeply hurt and alienated brother, though he would not discourage her visits. Of course, younger sister and I were too young at the time to recall much, except for some flashbacks embedded in my mind. However, the fact remains that these two events—our father's death and then the presence of this "step-father"— the murderer of our father—were most catastrophic and they drastically impacted our lives.

What were the consequences upon our lives from this new entry in our lives? The individual who murdered my father was now our "step-father!" Frankly, I have a hard time bringing his name to my lips, let alone write it down; it is impossible to think of him without intense inner agitation, anguish, and pain. His entire family clan were relatively uneducated, culturally decadent, artisan-types, and many engaged in blue-color jobs. God knows–I am not at all the class-conscious type, but the fact is that this individual and his relatives, many of whom lived in the same neighborhood, lacked in education except the most basic, and, in general, their character and behavior hardly ever reflected any cultural refinements or conscience. This individual fully reflected that background. Being the only son in his family of six siblings perhaps had a great deal to do with his narcissistic character. He grew up as the favorite, "spoilt" child, who could get away with about anything, even murder, in an environment where he would view his bestial passions with pride. His formal education was about sixth-seventh grade level. Given the times, he had a fairly luxurious private bedroom room on the second floor of the house where his first wife and children lived; the house was next to ours. There were occasions when I observed him, despite my young years, engaged in alcoholic drinking— something absolutely forbidden, religiously and culturally.

This individual operated one or two passenger buses and he himself used to drive one; that was the source of his livelihood, and apparently earned well at the time. The individual was known as a domineering neighborhood bully, a macho-type, an occasional drunkard, a womanizer, a vicious wife-beater, an abuser, absolutely lacking in what one would call the most basic traits of being human, with no fear of God or his own mortality; these are the things I came to observe about him as a youngster and more as I grew older.

3. My Memories Till Age 10

At the time of this new household (August 1941) emerged, I was less than five years old, and I lived in this environment till age 10. Even during those tender years, I observed so much, and much of it is stored in my memory. I was unable to react to my experiences, even in the mildest manner, only quietly absorbed and suffered. I was supposed to be the obedient and respectful "son" to the "step-father," or else risk his wrath. While I was not fully conscious of all the circumstances, I do know I always held utmost contempt for the individual. However, throughout my first 28 years of life, till my marriage in 1965, I had to live a torturous double-life, a lie that I had to endure and for which I still suffer from self-hatred and nightmares; this was the expedient thing to do at the time for the greater good of the family. However, the horror is so deeply entrenched that I still wake up drenched in sweat, screaming; I see the monster. My wife would try to calm me down. "It's okay, it's okay; it is only a dream," she would say. "We are safe. It's just a dream." I would calm down and then try to go to sleep, trembling.

I recall that, before and after this marriage, we traveled to Jullundhar on more than one occasion, sometime staying in the house of my aunt (my mother's young sister, mentioned earlier) for a few days. During these rendezvous, I don't recall if my sisters accompanied us, but I used to be along; and the "step-father" was always there. What were these trips all about, God only knows—but my mother's alliance with her sister was always there, and so was the apparent deceptions about all these links that were developed with my maternal uncle. He was kept in the dark as to whatever was transpiring.

I remember the room where we used to stay at our aunt's house; it was on the outer fringe, on the left side of the entry-door. I remember too that in this house, once or twice our suit-cases (metal trunks) were broken open and some of our belongings were stolen. These thefts happened with the complicity of those with whom we stayed, especially the male adult who lived there and who had an openly-secret amorous link with our aunt. During these visits, I remember we would also visit our uncles, but without the company of the "step-father," for whom the uncles (my mother's brothers) had utmost contempt. In fact, I don't remember if the brothers ever shook hands with that individual; for them, he was a non-entity.

Also, during these visits to Jullundhar, my mother was persuaded, against the advice of her brother, to lend a significant sum of money to her younger sister; this was part of the estate left behind by my father. That loan was never returned, despite the frequent and dire needs for various basic necessities for children, including myself. But perhaps some good came out of this 'lost loan' later in my life, as will become apparent.

And personally, what all did I experience, observe and absorb during these early years? Much too painful to recall, but recall I must for this odyssey. Of course, there was enormous jealousy and contempt, naturally, from the "first" wife and her relatives; and, naturally, this contempt would also often transfer to us, the children of the "second" wife. We continued to live in the same house where once my own parents lived—a small house, with one sitting-room (where my father died), small courtyard, a large room where we all slept during the winters (upstairs on the open roof during summers), and two other smaller rooms, both used for storage, etc. Around this house were the houses of the "first" family ("first" wife, four children, etc.), as well as the houses of this new character's sisters and their families, etc. Also, there were some Hindu families in the neighborhood. All of these people knew my father well; in fact, he was a teacher for many of the neighborhood children.

And it is in this house where I experienced about the most traumatic episodes of my early life. The "step-father"—let's just call him what he was, the "beast"—was about the most brutal man. For in his character and behavior, even as a youngster I could sense, there was no conscience or humanity. His rage and most abusive outbursts about the smallest things would be uncontrollable and so frequent. The house was a house of terror and everyone lived under intense fear as to what might happen next and how he would abuse, physically and emotionally, not only our mother, but each of us children. At the time of the August 1941 marriage, my eldest sister was a teenager, about 15, another sister about 9, myself (about 4), my younger sister (about one).

So quite routinely, what I saw was horrible and so painful to recall. He would spring on mother just as a tiger attacks its prey. He would catch her hair, throw her to the floor and kick her in the body with his shoes. And beat her to pulp in the most ferocious ways—using his hands, feet, sticks, and whatever else would be handy, physically drag her from one end to another by holding her hair. He would even drag her and dump her in the street. And often she would bleed profusely from her mouth or nose, or from injuries elsewhere; she would have black and blue spots on her body from the beatings. She would cry and cry and scream and scream–and yell out loud for help from anywhere. And we the children would helplessly watch, cry, and scream; I distinctly remember my own helplessness and crying and screaming. And if we would want to intervene and try to protect our mother from the abuse, then we too would become the targets of his beatings. Scars on my body are constant reminders.

I remember often I would crazily run, while crying and screaming, to various elders in the neighborhood, begging and pleading for their help–to save my mother from the hell she would be experiencing. Sometimes someone would intervene, other times none was forthcoming.

And, there were the bestial deeds by the monster that I saw and which arouse enormous self-hatred in me; and I suffer and agonize. With my young eyes, I saw the beast abusing my sister. We were under the narcissist's control and here was a man with no conscience or morality whatsoever. Our mother was helpless and forced to accept his satanic deeds. While still under 10 years of age, I could understand but helplessly suffer. I have always wished if there was a way to have part of my brain removed so those memories would vanish forever. And the pain always persists and lingers. Perhaps my other older sister, teenage by 1944 or so, also suffered. But, surely, she too observed and endured a great deal in that hell of a house. I often wonder if it was her inner torment that caused her to suffer from tuberculosis at a young age; she died in July 1947, at the age of about 16. And I would always worry, lest the beast might kill me in his rage, for, even at this young age, I had seen so much of his beastly behavior; and he knew.

Then there was this noble lady who, with her family lived in another neighborhood, about a few blocks away. That was a very decent, noble farming family; I remember them well. That lady was my mother's confidant and knew rather intimately all that my family had encountered, the circumstances surrounding my father's death, and whatever else transpired after. This lady was sometimes the savior of our new household's calamities. Often when others would be reluctant or not available, I would run to her house to seek help.

Once I remember when at about age 8 or 9 (perhaps 1945 or 1946), I had been circumcised, and because of the fresh incision, I would usually be wearing a shirt and no pajama or underwear. And, oh, how I so vividly remember! Once the beast was mercilessly beating my mother and dragging her back and forth by holding her hair, kicking her out of the house; and I can still hear my mother's screams, and those of my sisters. And I remember how, half naked, screaming, and beating my head out of anguish, I ran, despite my incision and wearing no trousers, as fast as I could, to that lady's house so she could immediately come and save my mother. God bless her soul–she did come and intervened; I don't remember much else. But such were the routines of our life in the shadow of the beast; we constantly lived in fear of his terror. These realities, fixed in my psyche, become so fluid with the slightest jolt.

During this time, I was attending school, Phillaur Primary School, about a mile away from the house; and I would walk to it, sometimes alone, sometimes with other children. And the beast had little in terms of financial resources and there were two families to support. The man knew well that my father had some assets, including two small rental houses in Jullundhar; and there was also some of my mother's jewelry. Now, of course, that rental income belonged to him for whatever he pleased to do with it. Certainly, that income was hardly available for the well-being of the rightful heirs—the orphans of the family. Given such economic circumstances, we hardly had anything even for our most basic needs–food, clothing, shoes, etc. We were lucky to have bare-bone three meals a day; and a little meat and a glass of milk were rarities. Going to school hungry or going to sleep hungry was not uncommon for me.

And, to supplement household resources, my mother made use of an asset she had received at her first marriage—a sewing machine. In addition to other household chores, she would also sew or stitch clothes for others in the neighborhood and thus earn some extra income. She was forced to make use of that sewing machine, as a source of income, throughout the years. I remember sometimes I would be sitting next to her or leaned against her, and curiously watching her operating the sewing machine—and some time she would ask me to thread the needle for her! And I remember walking to school in rather torn-down chappals or sandals, sometimes even barefoot. But schooling was a must–my mother was so keen about it, for I was the prodigal son, the potential 'savior' of the family, the old-age security, and to carry the name of my murdered father. And it seemed like, with God's mercy, I was a bit driven and motivated; perhaps it was the force of circumstances, or whatever. And at a rather young age, I jumped one or two grades.

And during those childhood years, one of the chores that I had to do almost daily was to take the "step-father's" goats to the neighboring farming area (about a mile away) for grazing; and that's when I also would encounter poisonous snakes along the way. As for "fun," there was hardly any time. I would rarely play with other children and when I did, I did not have much to share with other kids. Who could buy me some games to play with–marbles, kites, balloons, etc. I was the forlorn, lost orphan, bewildered, and buried in my traumas—and perhaps subconsciously yearning to be saved somehow. And there was this sense of loneliness, with none around me whom I could call my father; and also because the other boys were often a bit older, bigger and intimidating. And then, I remember, I always felt sorry for being fatherless; if I play with other kids, who is there to encourage me, boost my spirits? Who is there to compliment me if I did well in a sport? Or stand up for me if I got into a fight with someone?

I remember sometimes I would see other kids playing with marbles or flying a kite; I would just longingly watch them. And then at times, I would beg them to let me in a bit, for, "Look, I am fatherless; I am orphan!!" Oh, my God Almighty, those were the days; I was begging for their mercy. And even during those early years, I was a brooder, a recluse, a basically shy type, rather timid and an introvert; perhaps this was the result of my traumas and deprivations. But, I believe I was always keenly perceptive and observant of the world around me. Such was the environment that also coaxed me to seek genuine, sincere, and honest links with others; and I always yearned to reciprocate even with utmost self-sacrifice, God Almighty knows better. While pain was the rule, perhaps I realized at an early age that succumbing was not the option.

4. My Run-Away Escapes

And then during these early years, I looked for escapes from the environment of the horror house in which we were living—as though I was starving for childhood, yet hungry for life. And escape I did. I believe it was either in 1946 or early 1947 when I was either in the fourth or fifth grade. I ran away, twice, while still under 10! Somehow, I thought– perhaps quite rightly at the time–that I could escape to my aunt's house in Jullundhur and that household could save me from the beatings that I would often encounter from the beast. Indeed, there was also the intense hate I felt for that beast and what he was all about and what I had seen with my eyes in those years of my childhood.

So, I remember, I ran away from school, secretly boarded a train at the local railway-station, without buying a travel-ticket, holding my bag of books, and hiding myself in the train here and there so I won't be caught–sometimes even holding on to the outside bar and standing on the footboard of the moving train–and I was escaping to my Jullundhar sanctuary! Somehow, I reached Jullundhar railway station, and quietly managed to get out without being noticed by the ticket-checkers. And then I knew the couple of miles of walk to my aunt's house. My aunt's house was the sanctuary, but very, very temporary. Within a day or two, my mother and the beast came to get me; somehow, they suspected I was there; perhaps I might have given some clues–I don't remember. But, yelling and screaming, I was brought back to Phillaur.

And then–and then, oh my God, please help me, how do I say more? How do I bring myself to describing the rest of this saga! I was beaten and I was beaten–and I can almost see my mother and my sisters screaming, crying, and watching helplessly the physical and psychological torture of the only son and brother. And the beast tied my arms together and hung me to the top latch of the frame of one of the doors in the house, with my body in the air, as though I was to be slaughtered. And then the merciless lashing by the beast! I would wonder if he intended to kill me. I would scream, beg for forgiveness, promise not to run away again and always be obedient to him. My hate for him would multiply infinitely but it had to stay dormant and unexpressed. And the lie must persist.

Oh, God Almighty, please help me erase these scars from my memory—can't bear to remember. My children and my loved ones, please do know that I am not keen to burden you—I have carried it alone all my life. Please don't shed tears about what you are reading; those pains–and memories—are mine and mine alone.

(Accompanying is the picture of that door, taken when I visited the house in Feb. 2000).

Door-ledge of hanging and beatings as a child

Yet, even at that tender age of 9 or so, while I learned to be obedient, the rebel that had been created in me was still willing to take a chance again. So, after some time, I took the chance—and, once again, I decided to run away. I followed exactly the same path as before—took off from school, boarded the train, and secretly hung around the moving train so I won't be caught by the train officials. I made it again to my sanctuary at the aunt's house. At this later stage of my life, I can only reflect back and only imagine the torturous circumstances that would force a youngster to run away as I did, not once but twice. And, yes, the rest also followed. The beast, along with my mother, chased me to Jullundhur, brought me back, and yes, yes, of course–the hanging, the beating, the crying, the screaming, the fear of being killed, begging for his mercy, forgiveness, promising absolute obedience. Now, I suppose, the rebel had been subdued, my spirit was broken, my tiny body was shattered. I surrendered to my fate; I was now the helpless obedient slave. I suppose this too was the beginning of my double life: intense hatred for the beast within, and obedience and submission without, the later not only out of helplessness but also forced by the fact that my disobedience would cause the beast to be even more abusive to my mother and sisters—and me.

But, somehow I survived, though traumas remain. I learned to be more obedient to the beast, for he was all-powerful, controlling–he controlled us all; and how else he abused the rest of us, I don't care to remember; but there were abuses that these eyes watched and the body experienced and shed tears about—the abuses inflicted upon my mother and the rest of us.

During these years, I was perhaps a fairly diligent student. I know there were some teachers who, apparently having known my father as their colleague. showed special affection and care to me. One was a teacher in my primary school—always very sympathetic. Another was in the high school, who, as a colleague, not only knew my father well but apparently also knew the circumstances of his death. He would always show special affection and kindness to me, and I remember him especially well; I even recall his kind face. Perhaps it was the kindness and care of individuals such as these, plus perhaps the push from my mother, I was a diligent student, quick to learn, and progressed rapidly.

During these times, before migration to Pakistan, I would often go to the grave of my father; and my sisters' graves who were buried nearby. I knew the location of my father's grave in the city cemetery, adjacent to the local farms. Someone perhaps led me to it at some point or perhaps I remembered from memory. I remember I would go there often—either just glancing toward it while passing through when taking the goat for feeding at the pastures nearby. Some time I would stop by, just stand there and ponder over; or perhaps say prayers for God's mercy on my father's soul. I do remember that my father's grave was near the northern edge of the cemetery, almost at the point of entry, situated in a slightly hilly spot. I believe there was a marker with my father's name on it. After some time, however, because of rains or the nature of the terrain, the grave had sunken in the middle and no repairs were ever done; and that's how I remember it till today. I don't remember any other adult ever visiting my father's grave for prayers for his soul. Parenthetically, I might note, I went for a nostalgic visit to my birthplace in early 2000; more on my sentimental journey later in this narrative.

And, then, major political events took place in India, following decades-long political movements for independence from British colonialism. India acquired its freedom from the British rule in 1947 and on August 14, 1947, the sub-continent was divided into two independent nations–Pakistan and India.

Chapter II

MIGRATION, MY FOSTER HOMES, MY GROWTH

India achieved its independence from the British on August 14, 1947. The British had occupied the continent for over 200 years, and after prolonged struggles and sacrifices by the natives of all faiths and ethnicities, India acquired its independence from British colonialism. Accompanying the independence was also the division of the subcontinent into two independence nations—India (Bharat) and Pakistan, the latter to become a nation primarily for Muslims. And massive disruptions followed—over one million dead, 10 million displaced, 4 million Hindus/Sikhs migrated from Pakistan to India, and 6 million Muslims migrated from India to Pakistan. Even before the formal declaration of partition, extreme nationalism had arisen, leading to hatred, riots, murders of each other by members of various ethnicities, especially in areas adjacent to the proposed borders. About late August 1947, we migrated from Phillaur, now part of India, to Lahore, now part of Pakistan, about 90 miles away. I was 10 years old then; we were all refugees. And now began another saga of my survival.

After declaration of the partition, the bloodshed on

both sides became massively endemic. While the departing British had envisioned an orderly exchange of minority populations, the unanticipated scenario was just the opposite. Populations exploded into a cycle of brutality and retaliation, engulfing both new nations. Inflamed by religious/nationalistic extremism, blind hate overwhelmed individuals to annihilate the "other;" and these were diverse groups of people who had lived rather harmoniously for centuries. There were more Muslims desperate to migrate to Pakistan now, compared to Hindus and Sikhs who wished to migrate to India.

While migration began as a voluntary phenomenon, once the riots and bloodshed of ethnic purity erupted, it became a matter of necessity for survival and security. As communal riots worsened, Muslims must migrate to Pakistan, or else they won't survive; and similarly, for Hindus and Sikhs from the other side of the new border. Indeed, fanatics of one particular faith were keen to destroy followers of other faiths—Sikhs vs. Muslims, Hindus vs. Muslims in India, and Muslims vs. Sikhs/Hindus in Pakistan. While at first, elders of the Muslim community in our neighborhood felt reasonably secure and were not keen to migrate. However, as matters deteriorated, there was no choice but migration, albeit with the thought it was a temporary move and then everyone would return as things calmed down. That never came about, however.

1. Our Migration Caravan

And this is where, there was a most noble gentleman in the neighborhood, who also was an occasional savior for us when we encountered the beast's wrath in the family. He worked as a cook at the British-operated Phillaur Police Academy and he was instrumental in arranging our migration. Through his link with the British, a few buses were made available for many of us to be transported to Lahore, Pakistan. This migration happened late August 1947. Obviously, people took priority over possessions, except for the very basic necessities; there were hardly any possessions that could be taken. We all packed ourselves in a few buses, which were parked in the long drive-way of the Policy Academy. On both ends of the caravan, there were jeeps for protection, occupied by armed members of the British Gorkha regiment.

As the caravan began its 90-mile journey toward the newly-established border of Pakistan, near Lahore, I remember the conditions within the buses; people packed liked sardines, men and women tightly sitting on bench seats, while many standing wherever they could manage, including the footboard of buses And many were sitting on the roofs. Children were sitting in the laps of mothers, or squeezed on the floor near their feet. I remember sitting in my mother's lap, sometimes on the floor. There was continuous recitation of the Holy Qur'an and prayers for God's mercy and for the safety of our 90-mile journey. Window-shutters of the buses were closed or raised, for there were screaming rioters along the route, anxious to attack the buses.

And there were mutilated bodies of dead men, women, children, and even animals, scattered along the roadside and in the distance. The blind rage brought out the most inhuman instincts out of humans; there were body parts scattered all around. And, there were miles-long caravans of people—men, women, and children walking, frightened from imminent threats of being attacked and murdered, adults carrying children or older folks, people packed on bullock-carts, riding on donkeys, and domesticated animals walking along, all heading toward the promised land. And I remember too that on occasion I would innocently peak through the shutters and get a glimpse of the gory scenes, deeply engraved in my mind for ever; and my mother would scold me and push my head down so I won't see outside.

And I remember there were Sikh (and Hindu) fanatics along the road who would want to attack the buses and kill us all. And, once someone standing on the footboard of our moving bus was attacked and injured, but he did not fall off the bus and the bus kept moving along. What might have been our fate if the wounded man had fallen and then the bus had stopped to pick him up—and all of us would have been slaughtered. Gripped with intense fear and sounds of riots, gunfire, screams and cries on the outside, the 90-mile distance felt like a never-ending 900-miles. I remember too there was the eerie sight of dead bodies–humans and animals, floating in the bloodied ponds and lakes along the way and in the River Ravi, as we crossed the bridge that linked with Lahore. But, thanks God Almighty, our buses arrived safely at the border-town in Pakistan. Though absolutely destitute and helpless, we were "free" in the new land of our destiny.

2. Early Years in Pakistan

Once on the other side of the border, where do we go now? I remember we disembarked from the buses at Wagah, the border town in Pakistan, near Lahore. We spent the next three-four days and nights, living and sleeping in the open, under the sky, on the concrete floor near an abandoned gas-station. The elders would go around town, looking for some relatives or acquaintances who could assist. Apparently, they found some connection. Then, we all moved into a large, abandoned residential structure, located in Ichchra (a suburb of Lahore), with several autonomous units within it, a large entry gate, a courtyard in the center, and several abandoned shops on the western side of the building.

This was a Hindu/Sikh residential area (with Hindu or Sikh street names), but now taken over by Muslim refugees, as we were. These people, like us, obviously, escaped to the Indian side of the border, under circumstances similar to ours. God only knows whether they were assassinated by fanatics or whether they made it to the other side. I remember the residential units within this building had been looted and ransacked; the locks and latches on the doors were broken and twisted. There were some ordinary items of property which the new residents found useful in their new environment where life had to literally begin from scratch.

It was clear there was hardly anything in our new household for even barest survival; and there were two families to take care. The "step-father" was the head of both; there was his first wife, with four children; and there was our family, with two of us from my father and three half-brother/sisters. The extreme hardship of physical survival was such that, I remember, on more than one occasion, the women would cook some edible snacks, and accompanied by the older son from the first wife, we would walk the neighboring streets and hawk these edibles for sale. I wasn't much of a hawker and I wasn't in the lead–and I have no idea how successful we were. I do remember, however, if someone was not interested in buying our snacks, we would meekishly plead for a handout of some money. This episode of survival struggles, however, is always fresh in my memory as about the most demeaning expression of our survival instincts at the time; we were literally begging in the streets.

How we survived the next few months, I have little or

no recollection. But I do remember the "step-father," whose only useful skill was being an automobile driver, looked around for a job as a driver for some well-to-do, established family in the area. In due time, I remember, he did find a job as a driver; oh, how much fun it was to occasionally ride in an automobile with this driver! And sometimes we the children would even visit the bungalow of that family for whom he worked. And they would look toward us—the children—as their servants and occasionally even hand us some left-over crumbs of food, etc. I used to feel so utterly degraded, but those were the times.

In due time, some of my maternal relatives were discovered in Lahore, including my three uncles and the only aunt and their families. In the succeeding few months or so, these uncles apparently were able to obtain jobs, perhaps comparable to what they had in Jullundhur. Soon, my eldest uncle and his family moved to Rawalpindi where he acquired a job, but the other two stayed in Lahore. The younger uncle, one who was closely connected with us since the death of our father, also lived in Lahore. Our aunt and her family also moved into an abandoned house in the city; she was the confidant sister of my mother—and it was her house in Jullundhur where, before migration, I sought escape twice as a run-away child. In the ensuing weeks and months, my mother would visit these close relatives and seek guidance and assistance, especially from her youngest brother; this, of course, was the same brother whom she had often disappointed during those years around the time of our father's demise.

Later, however, our aunt and family moved to Karachi, where her eldest married daughter and her husband (a noble man who later turned out to be another angel in my life!) lived; the son-in-law was a fairly well-established businessman in Karachi. Both families lived in apartments (flats), opposite of each other, in an apartment building in the central part of Karachi. For my mother, however, the biggest concern was her orphan son's education and his future.

3. My Foster Home, Rawalpindi

For whatever reasons, however, I was viewed as a burden by the "step-father," even though he continued to receive rental income from the tenants who lived in our late father's property left behind in India. I was not to benefit from my father's resources. On the other hand, I was to be abandoned—and so it was! Who would feed me, cloth me, take care of my basic necessities? Above all, who would facilitate my education? This son of my late father was to be the "lottery-jackpot" for mother—and, thus, some minimum education—at least high school or matriculation—was most critical.

But how? I suppose after consultations with the brothers, sometime later in 1947, my mother took me to Rawalpindi, where I would now live in in the household of my elder uncle and his family; and I would resume my education there. That was my first foster family.

Looking back, I know how difficult things must have been for that aging uncle. I was an additional child along with eight growing children of their own, altogether eleven in the family. Obviously, survival with my uncle's meager income was most difficult and challenging. I attended Islamia High School, located close to the house where we lived; I completed the sixth-grade here.

Whatever the hardships, I was fortunate to have food and shelter and some emotional support, for I was now living with my first cousins. I remember, though, as a youngster, I yearned for the love of my mother. My father was removed from my life when I was four, and now at age 10, my mother was forced by circumstances to part with me, so I would get some schooling—and the beast was not willing to have me around; and besides, even if I had lived there, my education would have been impossible to pursue in the environment of that clan where appreciation of education was almost non-existent.

Life were extremely difficult in the new environment, however. Not only extremely crowded living conditions, but food was absolutely scarce–boiled rice topped with watery, lentil soup, swallowed down with water, was about the daily routine; and there were times when I was hungry and craved for food, any food. I remember I did receive some affection and care in this household, for which I am most grateful, yet there were times when I would sense some favoritism, I would feel like an outsider–and then I would sometimes cry alone, thinking of my own parents. I would often cry during the night, under my covers, in memory of my father and missing my mother. Given extremely cramped quarters, typically two or more children slept on each bed. And, I remember, sometime my stomach used to growl while trying to sleep—and I would cry and cry, for I used to worry if I was suffering from some disease that would kill me. Parenthetically, I should note that I did find, much later in life, that my other uncle—who had taken possession of some of my father's assets after his death—occasionally sent some money to subsidize my expenses while I lived in the household of the elder uncle.

And now another blow to my young psyche: my eldest sister's marriage had ended in divorce. While details of the circumstances are not quite relevant here, now she had to go back to the household of my mother and "step-father" in

Lahore; and that was the same environment where, before her marriage and before our migration from India, she suffered enormously, along with the rest of us. Now in this environment also lived my younger sister.

4. Another Foster Home, Karachi

It was around early 1948, my aunt and her family, along with the married daughter's family, came from Karachi to visit her elder brother and some other relatives in Rawalpindi. That's where I too was living at the time. Whether induced by some sense of compassion, or the guilt arising from the shared secrets of the two sisters, she arranged for another foster home for me—primarily the house of her daughter and son-in-law in Karachi. Or, the gesture might have been a payback for the never-repaid loan that the aunt had taken from my mother years ago, soon after my father's passing away. It soon became clear, however, that I was to travel to Karachi with my aunt and the rest of the family. I would live in the joint family environment there—the two families lived in two adjacent apartments, opposite each other, on the same floor, in Karachi. I would go to school there.

For a brief period, however, I do recall, we did live in my mother/step-father's dungeon of a household in Lahore, before moving to Karachi. Forced by the circumstances, my eldest sister also was living here, as was my younger sister. Of course, here too, I would observe and absorb the brutalities inflicted by the beast upon my mother—similar to the kinds that were stored in my memory from earlier years. Occasionally, the saving souls would be the beast's own sisters and that same gentleman, husband of one of the sisters, the noble man who also facilitated our migration to Pakistan in August 1947. The entire clan of the beast's relatives lived in the same multi-unit residential structure, formerly belonging to Hindu-Sikh families, which they occupied soon after migrating from Phillaur, India. And I was still living my double-life—intense contempt but reluctant obedience to the so-called "step-father."

After moving to Karachi, I recall well, I was utterly unhappy for having to part again from my mother. At that tender age of about 11 now, I terribly missed my mother and I used to cry so often. In retrospect, however, that was perhaps the best thing to happen for my distant future. And thanks Almighty, I had some shelter somewhere. As it turned out later, my two sisters would also move to Karachi in the same environment. Why? Obviously, there were fears of abuses on the part of that beast in my mother's life if they lived in that household in Lahore. And, besides, who would provide for their survival? In Karachi, my elder sister worked as a school teacher in a primary school.

I did find out later, however, that my primary benefactor would be the husband of my cousin-sister; what a noble human being he was. Whether he volunteered to help or was persuaded to do so, God only knows; the fact, however, is that, as I grew older, I always thought of him as an angel of a human being, a most gentle and kind-hearted man–and also a quiet but perceptive person, with a most generous spirit.

5. Our Living Environment

So perhaps around mid-1948, three of us—the two sisters and I—found ourselves living in Karachi, in the adjacent flats, on the same floor, in Karachi. Often interchangeably, we managed our survival either at our aunt's apartment or the apartment of her daughter and son-in-law. Our aunt's apartment had two small bedrooms and her daughter's apartment had three bedrooms. The couple was married well before India's 1947 partition and had lived in Karachi for a few years. This noble man was relatively well-off and had a successful import-export business. They had no children when we moved here. He was a thorough gentleman and a very kindhearted soul. His household included his wife and a servant. We three would usually sleep en mass on floors, along with aunt's five, almost grown-up children. And there was also that other adult male who had been part of the household from Jullundhur and now here as well. His presence always intrigued me, even as a youngster. But who was I to raise any questions? Besides, there were my survival instincts guiding me perhaps. Incidentally, I might mention that at this time my male cousin, perhaps in his twenty's, was employed in a government job and was the main source of income for the aunt's household.

As for the circumstances of my survival, there were constant reminders of the huge emotional gaps of my life. As an 'outsider,' I often felt deprived in terms of my treatment, especially in relation to others in the primary family, especially relative to my aunt's favorite younger son. If there were family chores to be done, often I would also be asked to take care. These included the frequent routines of going to the nearby stores to buy groceries and whatever other household needs. I recall my intense fear of being injured or killed when I would go out and squeeze through busy streets where there used to be unchecked traffic, both ways, of various types of vehicles—buses, automobiles, rickshaws, horse/camel driven carriages, motor-cycles, bicycles, and, of course, pedestrians. And there was also what I sensed was the injustice of how I was treated in terms of my survival needs; there was often the obvious favoritism of who gets what to eat—the best for the primary children, especially the favorite son; and minimal for this secondary orphan in the group. I remember sometimes I would be given my meal, sitting on the floor, in front of the kitchen, next to the servant. Intentional or not, treatment of that sort confirmed my lowly place in the family; and the memory has always haunted me. I should add that while I was given support by my relatives, I later discovered from my uncle's records that occasionally, he would send some money to subsidize my basic needs out of our late father's resources. I remember, however, wearing hand-me-down clothes, buying recycled sandals, etc. etc. Given the circumstances, it was all very painful to bear, though later in life I have felt a sense of gratitude.

It was perhaps late 1948 or early 1949 when the couple—my cousin-sister and her noble husband were blessed with the birth of a son. This was a most cherished, long-awaited event; and there was enormous joy in the family. Now another role was often expected of me–the babysitter for this infant. As he was growing, I would be asked to take care of him, carry him around and/or take him outside and engage in playful activities with him. If there were guests in the house, I would be the youngster's caretaker. My own childhood joys and needs did not matter; on the other hand, there were pressures for me to rapidly grow up and mature. And, indeed, there were pressures of studying; after all, pursuit of education was the supreme goal that had been set for me at this time. This was all while we lived in the center of the city and I was attending an ordinary school—one in which there were just a couple of rooms, heavily used and soiled mats to sit, and tin-roofs with holes. And when it rained, we would be drenched from leaking water. I finished seventh-grade here and then transferred to a newly-established high-school, about a mile away.

Thus, all along there was always the haunting sense of my lowly place in the family; and my enormous sense of deprivation constantly haunted me. I used to long how things might have been if my immediate family, including my late father, had remained intact, for, after all, I was the only son, now living as an orphan at the mercy of others. I remember how, at every step, I would think of my late father–how he would have wanted his son to be loved and nurtured. While other trials and tribulations of life may make them dormant, such gaps and scars never fade away. I remember I used to also miss my mother and often cry to be with her. But, the "step-father" did not want me in his household. Besides, my mother wanted me where I was, for she wanted me to finish high school (which meant, in the Pakistan-India school system, completion of 10th grade)—and be able to "stand on my own feet," meaning be employable as a clerk somewhere. I remember that she would tell the male elders of where I lived something like this: to get me to succeed in academics, do not spare the stick if that is necessary.

And the stick was not spared; beatings I would get, yes–from my cousin-brother. I remember geometry was my weakness, so I would pass the other two components of math—arithmetic and algebra—well enough to pass math overall. I usually did just fine in the other subjects. However, to ensure continued overall success, it was critical that I also improve my geometry skills; and that's where, in retrospect, the beatings from my cousin-brother were most helpful–and I am grateful. He helped me succeed in geometry, to the point where I began to enjoy the subject, and mathematics became my strongest subject, so much so that in the final matriculation examination (1951), I received a distinction in mathematics. Higher education was out of question, obviously.

While I don't quite recall the precise sequence of events,

there was the life-tragedy of my divorced elder sister. What future course of life for her? So, our mother being, naturally, keen to see her re-married, would often consult with her two brothers. However, for various reasons, that pursuit was unsuccessful. So the next choice for her was to be self-sufficient as an adult woman. She ended up enrolling in a teachers-training school to be a teacher at this time. This was the Government Training School for Girls, Sharaqpur, near Lahore. Our noble uncle financed the expense out of the reserves he continued to hold from my late father's monetary assets. His records, which I saw in his diary much later in life, indicate my sister attended this training school for two years, 1950 and 1951. Later, as will become evident, I joined her in Lahore while she worked as a teacher.

During this time, I continued to live in my foster-home in Karachi and continued my high-school studies. Meantime, my younger sister had been moved back to be with mother in Lahore.

6. My Growth and Maturity

Whether by the pressures of life in the various environments where I lived or the survival instincts from early childhood, I am known to be rather sensitive to things around me—and, God Almighty knows better, but I feel I have always been imbued with intense sense of justice, fair-play and compassion for others, especially the downtrodden around me. And again perhaps because of my early trials and tribulations, I feel I developed a strong sense of right and wrong from early childhood—always thinking through things by placing myself in the other person's shoes. I had to grow up and mature rapidly to adulthood, with my years of "living a childhood" literally lost.

Such background was part of the foundation of my links

with others—utmost sincerity, selfless care and empathy, and openness, whether relating with friends, relatives, or mere acquaintances. Further, I have been a keen observer of life around me, a fairly sound judge of others, with fairly decent ability to perceive, analyze, and reason out things. God Almighty knows best. Obviously, one can't be a judge of one's own personality—it is for others to judge.

Even as a youngster, I would often be drawn to reading books and short-stories that reflected the human condition in the society—poverty, injustice, religious intolerance, cultural/religious contradictions, rich–poor divides, etc. My internalization of such things served as critical guides to my maturity as an adult. And, perhaps most importantly, there was the guiding memory of my father. And, indeed, as mentioned in following pages, there was the overriding positive influence of some sincere friends and their families who took me as their own. In addition, I would collect quotations and sayings of prominent people to teach me and guide me—and still have that early-age collection in my 1958 diary. Some may be reproduced here:

1. The Four-Way Test: (i) Is it the truth? (ii) Is it *fair* to all concerned? (iii) Will it build *goodwill and friendship*? And (iv) Will it be *beneficial* to all concerned?

2. Faith: Nothing can hurt you in life so long as you have faith—faith in something, faith in someone; above all, faith in yourself and your destiny as an individual.

3. "Your tongue is a measure of your heart, so always be gentle"

And, in my latter life, both as a student and as an academician, I would always collect such observations and sometime develop some from own life experiences—and then appropriately share with students ("Food for Thought"), something meaningful that may guide them in their future growth. And I would also often place some on my office walls or office door. To some degree, they reflect my personality. Years ago, I enumerated many. Here are some of my favorites:

1. "A man's language is an unerring index of his nature"
2. "Practice random acts of kindness and senseless acts of beauty"
3. "Even when opportunity knocks, you still have to get up and open the door"
4. "Money may buy pleasure, but not happiness"
5. "Determination is borne in the crucible of adversity"
6. "Making a living is easy; living a life is the challenge"
7. "Success is not what you achieve; it is how you overcome the obstacles"
8. "Pursuit of a passion without compassion is mere obsession"

And I would often read (even write) short stories and poetry which would reflect upon the human condition, with all its injustices and insensitivities. And there were insights to be gained as to what real life was all about; and I had already experienced and assimilated some of that from my early age. I learnt at an early age that all individuals must, first and foremost, be viewed as humans, regardless of their status, creed, origins, religion, or ethnicity. That sense of universalism is deeply embedded in my soul. That sensitivity also often created enormous emotional grief. I could not bear to see man's injustices to others, or the misery of others less fortunate. There were times, I recall, when I would see a hungry beggar in the streets, I would want to help—but I could not. And then, in my solitude, I would grieve. That spirit of selflessness, that sensitivity, deeply ingrained from those early days, continues to be part of my being till now; and I say this with utmost humility.

All of this also meant, given the burdens of life imposed upon me at an early age, I developed an enormous sense of responsibility and conscientiousness, whether it is a task to be voluntarily undertaken, or as my moral-ethical obligation to someone, or a task that is part of my job responsibility. Also, I learnt to be rather well organized and meticulous about details, whether the focus was on my personal affairs or duties of a job.

Those characteristics became intrinsic parts of my personality, as I matured into adulthood; and they were most critical in what success I had in my employment and other pursuits in Pakistan. And those traits also played a huge part in enabling me to overcome various hurdles that led to my coming to the USA to pursue my dreams of higher education and then to succeed as a student. I can honestly say the same concerning my interpersonal relations with others—whether friends, neighbors, colleagues, students, or people generally. And, I must humbly state that over the decades, I have been most fortunate to have lifelong, sincere relationships with scores of people, young and old. Some have responded to the call of their Maker, but many others survive till today and I am often in touch.

Chapter III

MY SCHOOLS, MY FRIENDS

I was shifted to my second foster home in Karachi in 1948 and, along with my two sisters, we lived there for almost three years in the household environment of our aunt and her daughter/son-in-law. There were my aunt's five children, the youngest about 7-8 years old son, the most favorite. We were welcomed, but I quickly sensed how we would fit in the hierarchy. Yet, gratefully, we had shelter.

My older sister found a job at a nearby girls' school, where the younger sister also resumed her studies. More critical was my education. Where do I go?

1. My Tin-Roofed High-School

There was a nearby school, a small, very temporary, ordinary structure, with porous tin-roofs, barely shielding students from rain or the heat of sun. There were no chairs or desks; we sat on ordinary rolls of jute mats, with holes and tears. There were perhaps a total of 10-15 students. I joined the seventh-grade at this school; this was sometimes in the second half of 1948.

While I studied here and finished my seventh-grade here, this was hardly a school. This is where I met one of my dearest friends, Mushahid, whose circumstances were about as dire as mine; but he had his loving family of parents and other siblings. And I felt so welcome with all of them. He lives in Karachi, and we continue to be in touch frequently.

2. High-School Proper

And then, as it turned out, the temporary school closed. There was another more authentic high school, about a mile away from where I lived. I passed their qualifying test and was given admission to pursue the remainder of my high school grades (8th through 10th). This school had a credible corps of teachers for various subjects. There were specialized subjects, taught by specialized teachers, with separate rooms for students of each grade and appropriate subject level. There was a well-qualified principal for the school. There were about 200 students.

My friend, Mushahid, also transferred to this school. Along with so many other friends, here is where, perhaps early 1950, I also met another dear friend, Asif. Given our common social sensitivities and literary interests, this friend and I developed a very special affinity. His family also always extended utmost love and affection to me—gestures that I used to yearn for so much at that age. I was very much like another family member in their household.

3. My Friends and Student Life

Obviously, there is more to my interpersonal links during these years in Karachi, outside the household where I lived, especially with those friends. We three were in the same grades together, and often in the same subject-classes. Mushahid and his family had migrated from Aligarh, India, and lived in a modest dwelling, not far from where I lived. It was soon clear that, while there was a lot of love in the family, economic survival was a real challenge. The entire family was very affectionate toward me; that affection–plus our shared problems of survival–nurtured our friendship for the rest of our lives. Mainly because the space where we lived was too limited, this friend and I typically studied together in an alley adjacent to his house, below a staircase, usually under the light of a kerosene lamp; electricity was not readily available and if available, it was too expensive.

And there was also the close friendship with the other friend, Asif, whom I met in our 8th-grade at the high school; this friendship too has prevailed throughout our lives—extremely close, sincere, selfless, and undoubtedly this link, along with that of his entire family, turned out to be about the most significant source of encouragement and inspiration for my future life. We three always stayed in touch, wherever located.

But who was this friend of mine? Asif and his family–parents, six brothers and three sisters –migrated from Hyderabad Deccan (though originally from Delhi, India) to Karachi in late 1949. His family too faced enormous economic difficulties, but like my other friend, they too were very close-knit, loving family. There was such strong affinity among the three of us. We bonded together as the best of friends–sincere, loving, caring, affectionate, understanding, compassionate, and sacrificing for each other. We would share with each other all that life had given us to experience at this young age, especially this fellow–the emotionally-scarred, traumatized youngster, deprived throughout from the love of his own parents. They did not have much materially, but they had all the love of caring parents and family; and I had neither. Soon they discovered all about me–where I was situated, my aches and pains, beginning from my very early age; and these families substantially filled the gap for me. I am so grateful.

I must confess that I often had a tendency to open up my book of life with others who seemed sincere and trustworthy, for I was so desperate for loving relationships. Given what life is, I often found others who also had their own tragedies. Such circumstances strengthened my bonds of friendship with many whom I encountered. However, we three bonded together the closest. Since Mushahid lived nearby, I would often visit him, especially to study together. And his father would refer to me as Beta (son), and that was so soothing for my ears, and he always spoke to me so affectionately, as did his mother. Sometimes, they would invite me in to share food with them; simple as the meals used to be, but there was so much love.

Asif's link, however, became a special part of my life, and it was so mutual. He lived a few miles from where I lived, but sometimes I would go by bus to see him. His elder sisters attended a college near where I lived and sometimes he would escort them; and then he would also visit me at the apartment where I lived. Soon he was known to all the family members with whom I lived. We always enjoyed reading literary journals and short-story books; and we often shared each other's concerns and anxieties.

Soon after migration to Karachi, Asif's father–what memories, what a wonderful human being—established a small printing-press business in a central part of the city. With a large family, there were huge economic difficulties. Next to this facility, there was a milk-yogurt-shop. Sometimes Asif and I would end up at his father's printing shop–and his father would approach me with such affection, the "beta" (son). He would always insist that we both must have a yogurt-drink before departing. There was seldom much conversation with him, but what little there used to be, it was always imbued with much fatherly affection; it would move me so intensely and draw me even closer to this friend and his family. And soon I discovered very genuine affection from other members of his family; I was like another son for his mother. And soon I also discovered that we were inseparable; we were so innocent, so naive, so selfless; and we felt our lives would be unfulfilled without each other's friendship. And it was so pure and noble; we were so lucky.

But we were still high-school students, and now in the final year of our tenth-grade matriculation and the year is the second half of 1950 and our matriculation exams would take place in March or April 1951. We continued to be closely connected. Our most important concern at this time, however, was preparation for the exams. Each of us was in a situation that successful completion of high school was an absolute necessity, for without that, each would encounter quite formidable problems, especially true for me, the youngest of the trio. Asif must get through, for there were several other brothers and sisters in the family and, while there is lot of love, that love alone won't feed the family. Economic conditions were extremely tight; if he fails, obviously there would be added burden on the family resources. And Mushahid must succeed; he is the eldest son and once he completes high school, he could find some job somewhere and provide economic support for the family (an unmarried elder sister and two younger brothers, plus the aging parents); going on for higher education was not an option.

Regardless, those dear friends of mine had their loving, caring parents. and brothers and sisters, so if they failed, there was the family love for support and comfort. However, as for me, failure was simply not an option; if I failed, where would I go? Who would be there to comfort and encourage me? Who would support me in the next year? Would the family folks where I lived provide me shelter and support next year if necessary? It was already quite clear to me that there was to be no more education for me beyond high school. I must succeed now; and then I must enter the job market and start earning a livelihood to support myself, my sisters—and, yes, also to subsidize the "step-father," my mother and other siblings, all living in Lahore. This last subsidy was always a painful necessity, for the sake of my mother; without it my mother would suffer at the hands of the beast; I was still living the lie of my double life.

And, as we prepared for the examinations, I remember we all used to pray for each other's success. My two dear friends would tell me later they used to specially pray for my success, for failure would likely leave me stranded in life, possibly nowhere to go, possibly the remainder of my life without even a high-school diploma. The hell of my future would possibly be worst than the hell of my past.

We studied hard and prayed hard. We took out matriculation examinations in early 1951, administered by the Karachi Board of Secondary Education. And then we anxiously waited for the results. There were moments of desperation; we would connect with each other as well as other friends and discuss all sorts of scenarios of our future. During this time, I remember, since going to college was not at all an option, I started learning typing at the neighborhood type-writing training institute, for such a skill would be instrumental in finding a job, assuming I passed high school. Before too long, the results were declared—printed in the local newspaper. God Almighty was most kind to me; I passed, I passed; now indeed I was a high-school graduate. My mother's prayers answered; now I can stand on my own two feet; I could get a clerical job somewhere! However, most painfully, my two dear friends did not make it, nor did some other friends whom we knew; I was the only one to succeed in our group. My sense of relief, however, was overshadowed by the fact that my dearest friends didn't succeed. Indeed, God must have had a special eye of mercy toward this orphan. And I remember thinking of my late father—how proud he would have felt about his son's success. I missed him terribly. And I grieved for my two dearest friends who had failed. Yet, as they told me, they were happier for me, as compared to their own agony.

Perhaps a brief note about the kind of youngster I was evolving to be—i.e., in terms of my character, my aspirations, my sensitivities. Missing in my life, almost throughout, was the fabric of love that any young person needs for healthy emotional maturity and security. Under such circumstances, it was easy for a youngster to become a rebel, a rascal, a street urchin, perhaps even a criminal mind. Somehow, I was able to overcome such negative temptations; perhaps there was the subconscious urge that I would not want to disappoint my late father; or, the positive influence of close friends and love from their families. Perhaps this was also the result of some far-sightedness that persuaded me to try to stay on the right path. My circumstances denied me my childhood, but my epiphany forced me to mature rapidly. While still a youngster of 14-15, I had to grow up and mature rapidly, for I was soon to move on to the adult world of work and responsibilities.

Such circumstances also meant that I often looked for caring, sympathetic adults. And I found several friends and associates as I entered the world of work at age 15 or so. Some of these friends had their own stories which would cause them to empathize with others. "Do unto others, as you would have others do unto you" has always been my guiding principle. And a deep sense of fairness and justice has always been at the core of my heart and soul.

Oh yes, there is an innocent, hilarious event that must be mentioned. Once during these years, I remember, my dear friend, Mushahid and I had a falling out—and it was intensely painful for both. And there was our youthful ego as to who would make the first move to reconcile. Much later in life, he told me how he used to long for our reconciliation, so he took some concrete steps! He told me he used to come to school and also visit the street where I lived, wearing a special 'surma' (a powdered potion) in his eyes. The idea was that when there would be eye-to-eye contact between the two of us, I would be so affected and softened that we would once again be close friends! What naïve, noble innocence! But, whatever it took, that potion or something else, it worked; and there was never any love lost; we were soon friends again—and have been ever since.

More importantly, what next for my future?

Chapter IV

POST-HIGH SCHOOL, LAHORE AND BACK

Having overcome some major obstacles of my life, I was fortunate to have achieved a key milestone: completed and matriculated (high-school). Higher education was hardly an option at this time. But what next?

I used to think of perhaps joining the Pakistan Armed Services and aspire to be an official of sorts; air-force offered good salaries and it had a lot of glamour. But I found out that I was too young (only 14+) and a 110-pound weakling to even bother. At the same time, however, there was some encouragement from my uncle, located in Lahore, about the possibility of my college education. He indicated that if I were to move to Lahore, I could possibly be admitted to a college in Lahore, and he would assist me financially from my late father's resources in his possession. Also, some of his friends would guide me.

1. Higher Education: Move to Lahore

I moved to Lahore about mid-1951. My elder sister was at this time employed as a teacher in a school in Lahore and living in that demonic environment of our mother's household, with "step-father" present. After my arrival,

50

living in that environment was no longer an option. Perhaps with the help of her brother, our mother explored some options for our shelter elsewhere in Lahore. We were aided by the grace of a distant-relative lady who lived near the house of our uncle, my mother's brother. The lady lived there alone, while her daughter's family lived away at the location of her husband's job; there was room for us to be temporarily accommodated. This house was just opposite to the house where our uncle's married daughter, her husband and family lived. However, perhaps our precarious circumstances did not warrant any linkages on their part with the two of us; we were ostracized—no connection, no link, even though we two were close relatives. Amazing how the worth of humans is measured; much, much later in life, when I was reasonably well-established in life, it was a different story; they were so respectful and anxious to connect.

During this period, I often connected with my uncle, who lived nearby. He was sympathetic and inclined to guide me in furthering my education. He connected me with one of his acquaintances to assist and guide me. As it turned out, that individual was a rascal of another kind; I was a youngster and I felt, to be helpful, he wanted to abuse and exploit me. So, I was discouraged from the education plan. In the interim, I recall, I joined a typing-training institute in Lahore, so that my time is not wasted; I had, of course, learned the basics in Karachi earlier. During this period, my dearest sister was my surrogate mother and supporter.

All of this was happening in the second half of 1951 while I was merely 14 years old, approaching 15. I remember too that while living here, I was physically maturing into the age of puberty. And, in retrospect, this is hilarious. Not knowing anything about the transition, I worried intensely as to what was happening. Was I becoming sick of some terrible disease? I remember, though, thinking about my late father; I wished he were in my life so I could inquire about the physical changes I was encountering. I soon discovered, however, that my changing physiology was part of the natural phenomenon of masculinity.

While living in Lahore, I would occasionally connect with my mother; after all, she was my mother and also living there was my younger sister. And, of course, whatever my future, there was also that beast to whom I had to pay respects and convey my obedience. I would sometime observe the beast enjoying liquor drinks in the company of his friends, with doors closed. And my mother and the beast would long for me to "become something," now that I have completed high school. And they were not too keen that I should go on for higher education, for obvious reasons. During these trips, I am not sure if my sister accompanied me. Much later, I discovered, that there were times when I would come to see my mother, but the beast would, under some pretext, not let me see her; he won't let me into the house. She suffered; I suffered.

While living in Lahore, I remember I would exchange letters with my two best friends in Karachi, especially Asif. Somehow the friendship was more continuous with Asif and the link a bit stronger; he was about the closest chum to always share and console. He was quite the literary type–sensitive and perceptive to his surroundings; he understood the agonies of my young life well and I used to feel as though his friendship with me was more reflective of his concern for me and for the web of life that entangled and strangled me. I remember we would write letters to each other–and the competition was whose letter was longer and more expressive of our friendship! There used to be pages and pages of writing in each of our letters, very much in our youthful literary style, as though we were writing short stories revolving around our young lives. Incidentally, decades later, when we were blessed with the birth of a son in 1972, I named him Asif, after the name of my dearest friend.

2. Pressures of Survival: Back to Karachi

Before long, however, it was clear that my higher education aspirations would not materialize—at least not at this time. For one thing, the resources were not there; and then there was the other cost–what later I learnt to call, opportunity costs. After all, pursuing college meant also foregone income that I could be earning. And there were needs galore! Among other things, there was the pressure of my own survival; and there was the expectation of subsidizing my mother's household where also lived my younger sister and two half-siblings. The beast expected this–and I was supposed to be obedient "son." Further, my younger sister, about 12 at the time, lived in that environment; and there was the huge anxiety and responsibility about getting her married soon. My mother would worry intensely about the sanctity of her innocence, for there were vultures all around in that environment where nobility of character hardly mattered.

Then I ended back in Karachi, perhaps late 1951. My elder sister, the teacher, also accompanied me. And once again, we were living in the same two households (our aunt and her daughter's households) where we lived before—the same environment as we had left behind earlier. My sister found a job in a school; after all, she was a qualified teacher with credentials and experience; her income enabled some subsidy to the household expenses. I was once again linked with my friends; they were always there to share and care.

Both were students at the high school; they successfully matriculated in 1952.

By now, having continued my typing training in Lahore, I had acquired fairly decent typing skill; I could type at a speed of perhaps 50-60 words per minute. Also, I joined that same institute to learn shorthand; every evening I would go there for lessons. To be good at it, at least 6–8 months of complete dedication was essential. After all, typing-shorthand skills were known to be a relatively quicker path to finding a reasonable job—as some executive's personal secretary or assistant. While learning shorthand skills, I started looking for a job as a clerk-typist. Every day, I would walk up and down the commercial district of Karachi, exploring job prospects. Located in this area were commercial banks, automobile sales/repair agencies, travel agencies, and other sundry businesses. This area was also linked to the Karachi seaport area where Karachi Port Trust Authority and its offices were located.

And I am not even 15 years old yet and I am looking for a job in the adult world of work! Those were the demands upon my young life. Did I have a childhood? What is that?? I don't remember, but I have always wondered. I had to mature and grow up fast. Yet, in retrospect, when I look back at my life, I must admit I suffer from the pain of my scars, but for what God Almighty has endowed me in my latter years, I have no regrets. I know the accumulation of my traumas and scars also motivated me toward achieving some success in life. Here I am, in the autumn of my life, writing these lines; I have a wonderful wife, three wonderful children, and four loving grandchildren (Rafay, Kashif; Ariella, Nora). We are living a comfortable life—also able to extend a helping hand to some relatives and others, here and abroad.

But back to my search for a job as a clerk-typist. At this

time, one individual to whom I somewhat looked up to was my cousin-brother—the one who taught me geometry during my high-school days. He was employed as a clerk in a government agency and I used to envy him, for it looked like he could speak fluent English—and I could not! And everyone in the family looked up to him as the earning member of the household. He would guide me a bit about my job search. The biggest drawback, however, seemed to be my age; I was just a very skinny teenager whom prospective employers probably considered unfit for the adult world of work. But I had to persist in my search, for the economic needs were enormous.

3. First Job: Clerk–Typist

Job search required daily scrutiny, whenever possible, of the want-ads in the newspapers, as well as going door-to-door to visit various business entities in the city. In addition, word was spread to friends that I was looking for a job. I learnt that there was an opening of a clerk-typist position in an automobile-sales company. I applied and anxiously waited for a response. Through a connection, I learned I should come for an interview. My interview was for the position of a clerk-typist job that was advertised to pay Rs.150/- per month (about $30 at the time)–that was big, big money! I remember I went for the interview wearing the traditional dress—almost 15 years old, skinny, shy and timid teenager. I took the typing test and passed it; and I was interviewed by a supervisor. I presented myself as one who would be efficient, conscientious and responsible, willing to perform to the best of my abilities; I was desperate for the job.

However, I sensed that while I was qualified for the job, but I was too young. I beseeched and begged, pointing to my family needs and responsibilities. I went back and forth, so my desperation would be obvious to those in authority. Finally, they offered me the job, but, thanks, they offered me half the advertised salary—only Rs.75/- per month (about $15)! I readily took it. Look, mother and "step-father," and everyone else–now I have a job; I am able to "stand on my own feet!" I am rich!! And I will help you however much I can!!

I diligently worked at this job; but I kept exploring better prospects elsewhere. Also, I had continued my evening classes to further build my shorthand skills. About this time, I took a formal test, administered in Karachi, but sponsored by the London Chamber of Commerce. The test qualified me in shorthand proficiency, with distinction and a writing-speed of 80-90 words per minute. My typewriting speed was around 50-60 words per minute. Both skills were more than adequate for a decent job as a clerk-typist-stenographer.

4.   Another Job and "Nasty" Advances

And I was driven to move ahead. Through another contact, a good friend whom I remember well, I learned of a job possibility at the Karachi Port Authority. I applied and soon I had a job there that paid about Rs.110/- or so – a huge jump from that Rs.75.00—within a matter of just a few months. Given my skills and positive attitude, soon I was the personal assistant of a head-clerk in the KPT Storage Department. There were some amusing digressions here, worth mentioning. That individual was apparently "attracted" to my youthful, smooth-cheeked appearance; and he would sometime approach and talk to me in an awkward manner, unrelated to the job. And now my intense anxieties—my job and his suggestive advances! I was absolutely frightened and resisted my "boss's" advances.

Soon, however, the word got out that I was a competent, conscientious worker. And I was interviewed to be the assistant to the Port Authority's Chief Store Keeper, a rather senior position in the hierarchy. And he carried himself accordingly—impeccably dressed in a suit and bow-tie, and a pack of fancy cigarettes always at his desk or in his hand, etc. His office was rather huge, with a large glass-topped desk, two telephones, decorations on the walls, and a peon obediently standing outside the door. He selected me to be his personal assistant and I sat at a desk within the spacious area of his office. And, damn it, here too I was confronted with similar advances as in the previous situation. I remember this individual would sometime put his arm around me and touch me inappropriately. In his case, I was pretty sure he was the effeminate kind. I would resist but I was in a vulnerable position; the job was good and paid a bit better than the last job.

I would share these experiences with my friends, Asif and Mushahid–and we would find the conversations so amusing. How the three of us handled this oddball is another story. Just briefly, I accepted my boss's invitation to go to a movie with him. We conspired that my friends would be in the same move-house. The idea was that when at the end of show, he and I would be exiting, my friends would yell out appropriate vulgarities toward him, descriptive of what he was. That they did, indeed. Of course, I pretended innocence. Our hope was the individual would be reminded of his obnoxious character. However, I continued my job with him for a while—and survived!

5. Moving Up: Lloyds Bank Job

And then came another excellent break in my life. The year was perhaps mid-1952. Having been so close with Asif's family, there was his older brother—a college graduate, and an exquisitely polished, cultured young man. We all respected him a great deal; and he always conveyed a lot of affection toward me. Of course, that entire household was always a most welcoming place for me, far more than the environment where I lived. He worked in a clerical position at the British Bank, Lloyds Bank Limited. This was the Head Office of the Bank in Pakistan, with branches elsewhere in Karachi and other Pakistani cities. He knew that I had acquired respectable typing-shorthand skills and also that, among our friends, I had a fairly decent command of the English language. As a well-educated gentleman, he had rather good links with the Bank's hierarchy, so he told me of a job opening at the Bank.

I applied and passed the requisite typing and shorthand tests for the position. But then there was the interview with the Bank's British second-in-command, a tall, husky man, wore glasses, and had thick handle-bar moustaches, a rather intimidating figure. For this 15-years old rather timid youngster, who had grown up with the perception of Britishers as sort of masters of all the non-whites of the world, this was quite an interview–and it was in the English language! I distinctly remember how frightened I was. Thanks Almighty, I must have handled myself well enough and I was offered the job. And suddenly I was now earning Rs.150/- per month and working in a *British* bank, which, unlike local enterprises, had a prestige value of its own. Within less than one year, I moved from Rs.75 per month to Rs.150 per month! I was rich–and still only 15!

My job performance at this Bank was quite good, and I was well liked by the Britishers. Within a few months, I was promoted to be the personal assistant of the chief accountant of the Bank. I remember, after a while, I had my own desk in a corner of my boss's larger cubicle; and I was always there at his command (and the command was via the ring of a bell—in retrospect, how demeaning) at a moment's notice, to take dictation, to do his letter-writing, or whatever other chores were expected of me. I was a loyal, conscientious, hard-working assistant for him and he appreciated my performance. And my local colleagues looked up to me with envy. I was their link to the higher echelons of the Bank! I was climbing the ladder fairly rapidly.

Never content with my current situation, I always looked for ways to move up the ladder, with sincere hard work and dedication. I would see the Britishers as bosses; and also, I would observe the sons of Pakistan's elite being hired as trainees, to be then sent to England for further training, and upon return, destined to become senior officers, the local counterpart of the British officers. Much later, I realized this recruitment was predicated on the potential of future Bank business; upon return, these elite recruits would enhance the Bank's business with profitable connections. And here was this youngster of lowly background, acutely frustrated about the injustice of the situation: Why couldn't someone like me also aspire to eventually become foreign-trained official like them? However, the obvious fact was that I was not part of the country's elite; hardly. And that was a most painful feeling, for even at that stage of my life, I was thinking in terms of merits and merits alone. But then there was the reality. I would gently mention my hopes and aspirations to my British boss; and he would tell me—yes, perhaps, perhaps, I might someday be sent to England for training; but he was more confident of my becoming a senior *local* official in the Bank. Of course, the *local* official was not at all the same thing.

Yet, with hard work and diligence, I moved up the

ladder even further. Within the next few months, the Anglo-Indian female secretary of the Chief Manager, resigned to migrate to England; and then I was recommended by my boss to move into that position; this was probably during mid-1953. I would also be less "expensive" than what they paid the Anglo lady; she was probably earning well over Rs.300-400 monthly, whereas I would be content with much less; it was perhaps a little over Rs.225 or so, still a good jump over my previous Rs.150 per month. I moved into this role, with hopes of even higher salary later. Now I had an independent office, with glass enclosures, attached to the office of the Chief Manager. I had replaced an Anglo (albeit a woman!). That was the ultimate in prestige and status for a local! All my local friends and associates looked up to me with respect and awe; and God only knows—I can say with utmost humility, I maintained my links as before and never let pride get into the way. Now I had my own peon, attached to my office; but he was another human being, not my servant, I thought. I would ring the buzzer to call him for any chores–yes, just as my boss would ring a buzzer to call me to his office (number of buzzes determined whether his call was for me or his own peon!). In retrospect, it feels so filthy, obscene, and so terribly demeaning. But those were the days.

I remember the new boss was very impressed by my performance. Not only I was good in shorthand and typing, but often I would independently write communications for him. He would simply explain the contents and I would prepare a draft for his clearance; and then the final version would be done for his signature. And I was loyal and conscientious; I would be willing to stay late at work, if necessary. I was motivated to move on and to improve my lot in life. And I would also at times explore with my boss about my aspirations to someday becoming an official in the Bank. I would be given faint hopes, but not much else. It did not seem too encouraging.

During these years, of course, I was always connected with my friends, especially Mushahid and Asif. Asif was now a college student, but Mushahid was struggling to survive. He too had learnt typing by now. And I was now a rather respectable, well-placed employee of the Lloyds Bank, associated closely with the big chiefs. While I was attached to the Chief Accountant, I managed to persuade him to employ Mushahid as a clerk-typist. By this time, however, Asif's elder brother, who facilitated my job with this Bank, had resigned from his job and had proceeded to the USA on a Fulbright Award for higher studies. That was perhaps 1953 or 1954. We all admired him enormously; certainly, he was a role model for me.

As Mushahid joined the Bank, I regained the close association of an old friend and confidant who knew my heart and soul; and our friendship grew even stronger. Together we would dream of a better future; neither of us was content with our simple high-school education. But Mushahid had his own pressure of responsibilities–aging parents, an unmarried sister, two younger brothers, still in school; and very meager earnings of the father. And I had my own anxieties and concerns—and dreams Both of us had to grow up fast.

During this time, I would quite regularly also connect with Asif. While Mushahid and I were in the labor force and earning a livelihood, he was a student pursuing higher education. We would often get together. Before too long, the family had built their own house, Sajjad Manzil, in northern Karachi. But the contacts were quite frequent, and just as sincere, loving, as ever. Sometime I would connect with him near his college and along with some other friends, we would sit for tea in a nearby café. The entire family always welcomed me most affectionately–indeed, I had a home where there was genuine love; Asif's parents would often call me 'Beta' (son), a word that was always music to my ears. Certainly, I hardly ever heard this expression in the environment where I lived. His siblings were also very warm and affectionate toward me; I was like another brother in the family.

6. Part–Time College Plans

As for Mushahid and I, while neither was able to pursue college full-time, I would insist that we both must do more to improve our credentials and somehow use our meager resources for a better future. He seemed a bit content with the status quo, but I was rather pushy. We decided we would join an evening college and work toward a bachelor's degree. I persuaded him and we both joined an evening college, which was in the vicinity of where we lived. We paid the fees; but after a few weeks, we were discouraged and we abandoned. For one thing, the subjects, taught in the Urdu language, seemed rather challenging, and further, with full-time jobs, we were constrained for time.

Yet, I wasn't about to give up. Now I thought we both could perhaps do better at another evening college, located a bit farther but with English language as the medium, with which we thought we would be more comfortable. Unfortunately, this did not work, either; I know we wasted several hundred rupees in these attempts. Mushahid thought he would now try to work toward completing Bankers' examinations to enhance his position in the banking environment. And I decided to take some correspondence courses through a college, based in London. However, that too did not work for me. While higher education became elusive at this time, it did not become a lost cause. There were too many other priority concerns, mostly survival and family responsibilities. While I had my rather decent Lloyds Bank position, my plans for my higher education became rather ambivalent, though the yearning never stopped.

7. Other Responsibilities

During this time, we—the elder sister and I—continued to live in our aunt and her daughter's household environment. I worked at the Bank, and she had a job somewhere as a school teacher. She had gone through as a rough a time in her life, about as rough as one can possibly imagine for a young woman in that culture; only this brother—and none else—could feel her pains and sufferings. What was to be her future as a single woman? I used to wonder. In a system of arranged marriages, some elders must play the role and arrange for a suitable match for her. But who could play that role for her? And then there was the concern for my younger sister, a growing young girl, living in that den of scoundrels in Lahore.

And what were the various demands on my earnings during these times? I remember I would give my earnings, as the younger brother, to my sister, for she was like a surrogate mother. But our joint earnings required several monthly allocations: some to be shared with the household where we lived, some for my personal needs, and some to be set aside for younger sister's needs and some to be put aside for her marriage, whenever that was to happen. Of course, the "obedient" son was also regularly remitting funds to the household of the "step-father;" that was an absolute expectation. Since there was uncertainty whether the "step-father" would share any part of my remittances with my mother, I would also secretly send some extra money to my mother, via some confidant of my mother in the neighborhood.

Yes, this double life also meant that I would write "respectful" letters to the "step-father." And he would write "affectionate" letters to me, with ever-increasing demands for more help. And this was the man who had abandoned me when I was 10-years old and now he seeks my help! I had to comply, however, for the alternative was risking his wrath toward my mother. Those were the lies I had to live and suffer through for years. Incidentally, there was also a growing half-sister; and the "step-father," of course, expected that when the time comes, I would also finance her marriage.

Yet, despite a decent job, a good salary, respectable status and prestige among friends and relatives, there was this deep yearning for doing more with my intellect, aspiring for more education and broadening my horizons. And, in that connection, I sometime used to seek guidance from my uncle, the caring and compassionate brother of my mother who was intimately connected with our earlier calamities. One of my letters, written on June 1, 1952, saved in my archives, expressed my anxiety about losing time in pursuing my passion for further education and my dissatisfaction with my current status, essentially as a well-paid clerk, with no brighter future. Also, I talked about how to balance my educational aspirations and my other family responsibilities. My keen desire for higher education was always alive.

Meantime, however, I felt my job at the Bank was about as good as it would ever be. So, I continued to improve my lot by seeking other employment opportunities; and thank my stars, I was reasonably successful.

Chapter V

TRANSITION: JOB CHANGES, LIFE CHANGES

While I was comfortably situated at the Lloyds Bank (fairly good salary, decent job, good colleagues and friends, etc.), however, it was evident that my dreams of moving up the ladder would not go far; it was a dead-end situation. Certainly, my aspirations for higher education were to remain unfulfilled at this time. I looked for more challenging and better-paying alternatives. I remember my boss at the Bank discouraged me from leaving.

1. US-AID Job

During that time, the U.S. State Department agency–International Cooperation Administration, now named Agency for International Department, an extension of the U.S. Embassy in Pakistan, appeared on the scene, located not far from the Lloyds Bank where I was employed. I applied for a position there in 1955. I was a bit mature now, though still very youngish looking 18-years old; and I could communicate well. My interviews were successful and I was offered a job as an administrative assistant, with a substantially higher salary–about Rs.350 per month, compared to about Rs.250 per month at the bank; I accepted this job. The salary was even better than that of senior government officials.

The decision to take the ICA/AID job turned out to be the best of my life at that time. The working environment was far more congenial. I was a loyal, hard-working, diligent worker, with good work ethic. Soon, additional responsibilities were added to my job and I received decent salary enhancements. There was also overtime income and some other perks. The job often required interactions with senior Pakistani government officials and they usually seemed quite appreciative of my style and performance in my AID position. Those connections were most helpful for me later. Further, occasionally I would be invited in the homes of my American supervisors, something unthinkable with the Britishers at the bank. So here, I earned the respect and goodwill of three senior U.S. officials who were my immediate supervisors at various times and whose recommendations later were quite critical for my educational goals. I always feel very thankful for their support.

While employed here, my bosses had the confidence in assigning me a major administrative responsibility: to travel to Quetta, Pakistan, about mid-1957, and establish an AID office there for U.S. geologists to function there. That required the full spectrum of relevant tasks: finding and leasing an appropriate physical facility for offices; setting up offices with full facilities (furniture, supplies, etc.); recruiting a few local employees (administrative head, clerical and secretarial help, custodial help, drivers, etc.); leasing residential bungalows for the two U.S. geologists and their families who would be located here. Thankfully, all of this was satisfactory accomplished in a matter of about 4-5 weeks. Upon my return to Karachi, my bosses arranged a reception in my honor and acknowledged my "born administrative skills." I was most humbled; here I was—a barely 20-years old youngster!

What were my aspirations now? Same as before: not content with simple high school education, I must do something more to build my future. At my previous job at the bank, I was keen to move into their officer cadre and wanted the bosses to consider me for bank-training in England; now I was determined to pursue higher education in the U.S.A. Those dreams had to be put aside for now, however.

2. Other Family Developments

Here I am talking of mid-1950s. There was the responsibility of my unmarried younger sister, living in Lahore and there is also my elder sister, divorcee and single. Suddenly, around late 1955 or so, she linked up with the individual who lived in that joint household arrangement where we lived in Karachi. The two of them decided to get married; and they moved elsewhere in town. My sister did not consult about this decision with her immediate elders, nor told me about this choice. Making such decisions without consulting elders, or even taking them into confidence, is viewed strongly contrary to cultural norms; and my sister was ostracized. There was social condemnation for the "shame and dishonor" of this action, especially by the relatives where we lived.

Of course, she had a job as a school teacher, and he worked for that noble man's import-export business enterprise.

As a naïve young man, conditioned by the norms of the culture and influenced by the elders around whom I lived, I too joined the chorus of this condemnation. I was persuaded to disconnect with my "run-away" sister for her "shameful" deed. There was also condemnation from that monster in Lahore and I would get letters from him to join the ostracization of my sister. However, our mother understood the depth of the situation and she accepted this union. But, I abandoned my sister and her husband. In retrospect, it was truly one of the worst decisions I ever made in my life–and till this day, I continue to be ashamed and haunted by the guilt. I realized later, my sister needed all the compassion and understanding, not condemnation; I was dead wrong. Surely, she needed the love and understanding of her only brother, for whom, during earlier years, she was about like a mother. Both my sister and her husband moved elsewhere in the city and for quite some time I did not connect with them at all.

While all of this happened, soon my aunt and the family decided to move to a distant location in the city, though her daughter and son-in-law family continued to live in the same flat. And, of course, I moved with them and shared the expenses. My job continued with the ICA/AID at the same location, now a distance of about 4-5 miles that I used to cover by my bicycle. While we lived here, I regularly maintained contacts with my old friends. As for other interpersonal social links, it is worth noting that I often cultivated fond links with people considerably older; I would, I remember, often open some chapters of life with them, perhaps consciously or subconsciously with the motive of seeking their understanding. Also I would look for advice and guidance from these elders; some of them represented the substitute elders whose wisdom I missed while growing up; perhaps I viewed them as father-figures.

3. 'Jinn" Possessions Mystery

I lived in this household for the next couple of years. In addition to my aunt, others in the house were my cousins—two cousin-brothers and two cousin-sisters. My aunt was always the domineering, superstitious type, often consulting religious seers for advice. Here in the neighborhood there was such a seer who practiced his 'miraculous' activities. Soon, the family discovered, the elder of the two daughters was 'possessed' by a 'jinn' (ghost) and this was confirmed by the seer. He was supposed to be a good 'jinn' and a blessing for the family. He would 'appear' about every evening, communicating through my cousin-sister. It seemed a huge fraud to me, but young as I was, I was not sure. I would often talk critically and then I would be threatened with punishment by the 'jinn.'

Briefly, I decided to do an experiment to verify my own conviction. The experiment was simply that one evening, as the 'jinn' sat surrounded by everyone else, I claimed (falsely!) that I fell off the bicycle that morning in the middle of heavy traffic, as though the companions of the 'jinn' were trying to hurt me. And the sitting 'jinn' said, "we know, we know; this lad had been abusive of us, but we didn't want to hurt him—just warn him," etc. etc. I was quite amused; my experiment proved the fraud, but I could not say so, for I lived with the family and their belief was unshakeable. However, now I was convinced of the fake 'jinn.'

And, since I was often in poor health, aching body, and headaches, so my aunt decided to take me to the 'peer' to see if I too was 'possessed;' I decided to go along. The 'peer' tried hard; but every time, sitting near him with my eyes closed, he asked me, "Who am I?"—as though I too was 'possessed.' I would simply mention my own name.

Mentioning another name would have meant that was the 'jinn' who had possessed me. I was a disappointment.

4. Reconciling with my Sister

During this period, a major development took place; I reconciled with my sister. I began to re-evaluate my relationship with my elder sister—and the reasons why I had abandoned here. I don't recall the details, but I am sure there were some friends and others who assisted me in this re-evaluation. As I began to be emotionally drawn toward my sister, I remember, I was constantly drawn away by my aunt, for she continued to condemn what my sister and her husband had done. By this time, my sister and her husband were living in a room, rented from a friendly individual who lived alone in his two-room dwelling.

Before long, I connected with my sister and brother-in-law, and moved with them. Of course, my sister was immeasurably elated; she had her only brother back. Here, my sister gave birth to her eldest daughter, born in October 1955. This was my family now. I learned to reject the "shame-dishonor" notion of our culture. Now having fully appreciated with some maturity the background of circumstances, I realized my sister had been living an abandoned, lonely life, and given the circumstances, this marriage was about the best thing that could have happened in her life at the time. Now I was fully reconciled with my sister's marriage and her family.

And living in that one room arrangement was not easy. Soon we decided to move elsewhere and rented a three-room section of a house a few miles away. By this time, my aunt's household had also moved to another location. I would occasionally visit them; these visits were rather cordial. But none linked with my sister and her family; all of them continued to ostracize her. My friend, Asif and his family also lived in the same general area and we connected often; he was attending a college at this time. Since I was relatively "rich," I remember at times he would borrow some money for family needs; and I would always be repaid promptly.

5.   Trips to Lahore/Kasur

During these years, I would go to Lahore periodically and stay with my mother and the "step-father"–part of my continuous double-life saga. I would be welcome by the monster, now quite respectfully, for I was now his pretty good financier. One of these Lahore visits had to do with the marriage of my younger sister, perhaps in 1956 or so. This marriage for the young sister was a huge relief for me, my mother, and my elder sister, for she was now out of that hideous environment. I had, of course, financed the expenses, from several years of savings, perhaps also supplemented with some help from my late-father's resources held with my uncle.

During these Lahore visits, I would also visit my uncles—the eldest lived in Rawalpindi (whose house was my 'foster-home' during 1947-48, when I completed 6th grade there); another lived in Lahore. The younger uncle lived in Kasur, a town about 45 miles from Lahore; his family included his wife, and their young daughter, about 11 years old at the time. Of course, later in life, this young lady became my lovely wife; we were married in 1965. This uncle, youngest of the three brothers, had a significant role in our lives, as noted several times in this narrative.

This uncle would always welcome me and chat with me rather affectionately; and he would cautiously share with me some of the sordid episodes of our earlier family life. My mother always thought differently about her brother, however; she thought he had not been honest with our resources. On the other hand, decades later, I found documented evidence of his honesty and integrity in his diary. Once he borrowed some money from those resources. He expressed his guilt in his diary for having done so and asked God's forgiveness. And, in his diary, he wrote a note for his wife, asking her to replenish that amount, in the event something happened to him. Later, however, he replenished the amount and thanked Almighty God. Even if he had not replenished the amount, or even if he had made away with all of our resources, he could have claimed that during the hardships of migration, everything was lost. Obviously, he was guided by his conscience.

My uncle never ever visited my mother's house, for there was that murderer-monster whom he despised intensely. I would often talk with him about my dreams of a better future–more education, be a more literate person, go abroad, accomplish things to improve my life, etc. While he seemed content with what I had done so far, he would also be supportive of my aspirations.

6. My Dreams: Education Abroad

And now that my younger sister was married off, that was one less responsibility on my shoulders. So once again I began thinking of what to do with my life, for the job at ICA, well-paying and quite satisfactory, yet it seemed like a dead-end. While working here, I aspired to move up the ladder–and I worked hard and diligently; and indeed, I did move up, quite significantly, earning around Rs.800 per month when I left this job in August 1958. I was living a fairly comfortably, my main responsibilities were to supplement my sister's household expenses and to send some money (directly and secretly) to my mother's household, and, of course, to save for my future plans. Who knows–political situation could deteriorate and the U.S. AID offices could close shop. And then I might be left stranded. I was keen to enhance my intellect and potential. The goal now was to go to the U.S. for higher education, but that required successfully pursuing three challenges: admission at a U.S. university, obtaining a student-visa, and obtaining a Pakistani passport to travel abroad.

But who would admit me at a U.S. university, with only 10th-grade education? I would often go the U.S. Embassy's Information Center where the library included catalogs from numerous colleges and universities. Every U.S. higher-education institution required the equivalent of U.S. high school graduation for admission as a freshman; in Pakistan-India, that would mean two years of college beyond matriculation. So now I began vigorously using my energies and resources to seek admission somewhere in the USA as a freshman.

One of the things I did toward that goal was to enroll in a 3-credit course in Public Administration that was offered for senior government officials by Karachi University's Institute of Public Administration, which was run at the time by faculty from the University of Pennsylvania. My enrollment was almost impossible, for I was only a 10th-grade, high-school graduate, 19-years old youngster, and I was not even a government official. However, my bosses at the AID pushed my case and I was successful in the admission interview.

I enrolled in the semester-long evening course. And, despite competition from several mature, highly experienced, senior government officials in the class, I passed the course with a solid 'B' grade in a group of about

30 students. And the instructor gave me an excellent letter about my performance and potential that I was able to use to strengthen my U.S. admission applications. Further, my American supervisors and friends wrote strong letters of support. Some quotes are worth reproducing here.

(1) "I have known Mr. Ghazanfar for over a year and a half and consider him really one of the outstanding employees. He is intelligent, industrious, and has a pleasant disposition and would make a fine representation to the student body of Washington State University"

(2) "I have found Mr. Ghazanfar to be a loyal, hard-working, and intelligent employee. He has had an outstanding record of achievements with this Organization. A fine man and a true friend."

(3) "Mr. S.M. Ghazanfar has worked with me for about two years. In that period he has shown himself to be a young man with intelligence, ambition, honesty, and willingness to work hard and a nice personality. He has demonstrated real growth and I am certain that his capacity for growth has not been exhausted. Mr. Ghazanfar has been doing college work after hours and plans to do more. He will go far."

Given such endorsements, I was fortunate; I was accepted, as a freshman student, by three U.S. universities– American University, Washington, D.C., Washington State University, Pullman, Washington, and Berea College, Berea, Kentucky. I was perhaps the only one ever admitted in a U.S. institution of higher-learning with merely the equivalent of 10th-grade education; I have never heard of anyone similarly admitted. However, before they could issue me the document for the purpose of obtaining student-visa from the U.S. Embassy, I had to provide them concrete evidence that funding would be available for my expenses while enrolled as a student.

That was another challenge; there was none in the larger family clan who could provide me that kind of assurance; it required absolute, good-faith trust in me. The Embassy also asked for such assurance, for there was the risk that if a student was not self-sufficient, he could be a burden in the U.S. My only alternative now was to approach my friends and acquaintances, especially those well-placed in government circles. Through my job, I had cultivated several rather cordial such connections. Thankfully, some of them had trust in me. I gave them absolute assurances that I would not be a burden on them; and they were kind enough to trust me and they provided documents of financial support. And, then, indeed, I received the admission documents (the I-20 form)—and that was another huge first step toward my educational goals.

Next step was to obtain an international passport to travel abroad. And that indeed was another challenging bureaucratic ordeal at the time. Among other things, proof was needed that, being a migrant from pre-partitioned India, I was now a Pakistani citizen. Also, legal guarantee was needed to ensure that if I were to become destitute abroad, someone in the homeland would be willing to finance my return travel. Who would do that for me? Who would have the confidence that I would not allow that kind of situation to arise? Again, this step required trust and confidence in me.

Fortunately, same friends and acquaintances came forth who helped me earlier for the admission documents. One of them provided the legal guarantee needed; and others assisted by linking me with the appropriate passport-department bureaucrats so that the process would be facilitated. Eventually, I obtained the passport. During this period, I was also connecting with my friends at the travel office of ICA/ AID where I worked, to find a reasonably-priced one-way airline ticket to the U.S.A. Obviously, I was living frugally and saving resources for my travel, while also subsidizing the household in Lahore.

The final remaining task was that of obtaining student-visa from the U.S. Embassy. I had the I-20 admission form; I had the passport. However, the Consular Office needed to be fully satisfied with all the documents—authentic financial support documents, passport–guarantee document. And they also wanted an authentic personal document that assured full-financing for at least the first year of University expenses—and this had to be in U.S. dollars, obviously. There were some good friends at the central bank of Pakistan and at my former employer, Lloyds Bank. With their assistance, I was able to appropriate documentary evidence to the U.S. Consulate. And, thanks Almighty, the visa was issued. My hope and prayer, however, was to finance my expenses in the U.S. through part-time jobs and full-time work during summers.

I was now ready to embark on my noble adventure—to pursue my dream of higher education in the U.S. I had chosen to go to Washington State University, Pullman. My choice was driven by the fact that this university had granted me a substantial out-of-state tuition scholarship. Another reason was the knowledge that this university had an exchange program with a Pakistani Agricultural University and I thought the presence of some native students there would facilitate my adjustment in the new environment. Another was the fact that because of that exchange program, I had become acquainted with one or two faculty members from that university who were on visiting assignments in Pakistan.

I feel tempted to briefly recount the numerous blessings bestowed upon me thus far in my young life to pursue my arduous journey. Here was a lost soul, an abandoned street urchin, with none to guide or care, with no rich or well-placed relative–and even those who were there, hardly cared and unwilling to take a chance on me; only God Almighty was my Guide. And, of course, there was always the inspirational push from the memory of my late father, and there was the encouragement and inspiration from some friends and their families. Several major milestones had been accomplished for my sacred mission: obtaining admission at universities in the USA., obtaining financial guarantees from trusting well-wishers for admission, granting of visa, and obtaining the Pakistani passport; and also receiving a tuition-scholarship at a U.S. And sufficient resources saved for my travel. Everything looked on course, indeed. And I was ready to embark on my adventure in early September 1957, to join the fall semester at Washington State University.

However, as things transpired, there was a shocker. My travel arrangement could not be finalized on time. And I could not travel in time for the beginning of the Fall 1957 semester at the university I had chosen to attend–Washington State University, Pullman. Incidentally, all along I had assumed this Washington State University was located in the District of Columbia! But, having resigned my job effective August 1957 and unable to get to my destination on time, what would I do now? Where would I go? How would I survive the year? Somehow, with the blessing of God Almighty, after encountering enormous obstacles, I managed to be re-instated at the job. Now the target travel date was August-September 1958.

I was now ready to embark on the most significant and arduous journey of my life—travel to the United States for higher education, bereft with unpredictable challenges and opportunities. Will I be able to face the challenges? Survive academically and survive otherwise with my extremely meager resources? Will I be able to find some part-time work on the campus? Will I be able to send some money to help my mother's household in Lahore? What if I fall ill for some reason? What if I don't "make" it, then what? Regardless, here I was—a 21-years-old skinny young man, now ready to pursue an irreversible mission of my life, ready to take on the challenge of higher education, as a freshman at the Washington State University, Pullman, Washington

Incidentally, my mother and the "step-father," as well as my sister and several other relatives and friends, were not too excited about my aspirations, for I had an enviable job in Pakistan, with a very good salary. Being only 21, everyone thought I could eventually advance to higher places within Pakistan. So why bother to go abroad?

But, having worked so hard to put all the pieces together, now it was too late to turn back. Besides, I had only a one-way travel ticket to the USA. Once gone, I couldn't return, even if I wanted to! And, who would be there to help me with my return-travel even if I wanted to? Obviously, there was no alternative but to succeed—and succeed I must, absolutely.

Chapter VI

1958: THE AMERICAN DREAM

During those days, I used to keep a daily diary of major events in my life. I still have my 1958 diary, with so many memorable notations and quotations; some indeed served as useful guides for my life and living. I still glance through my diary nostalgically. Being familiar with so many success-stories in the land of opportunity, I was now ready to venture into pursuing my own American dream, the dream of eternal self-invention. Realistically, I anticipated that the American dream was not a sprint, nor a marathon—but a slow walk, sometimes with hurdles, yet with opportunities to reach one's destination.

I had all my travel documents—Pakistan Airlines ticket, passport with a valid visa, admission papers, etc. Before going to the airport, there was a gathering of friends and relatives at home, most of whom accompanied me to the airport to see me off. It was a tearful farewell; the obvious sense was that we would not likely see each other for several years into the future. All of them wished me well. In my mind, there was anxiety as well as the ecstatic sense of hope and confidence; I was determined to succeed. I used to always tell myself: One's destiny is in one's own hands, with God's help.

For my future successes and well-being, my mother had given me a paper with sacred prayers which I have always, till this day, carried in my wallet. Accompanying me was also a copy of the Holy Book that my friend, Asif, had given me as a gift; he also gave me a brief tape-recorded farewell message that he asked me to listen only upon reaching my destination; they are still my treasures. There was a suitcase full of essential clothes (including a heavy winter-coat that I had bought from a second-hand clothing store), three coat-pant suits that I used to wear to my US-AID job, and some cherished books and magazines, and a leather brief-case that I carried with me. There was some excess weight, but the Pakistan International Airlines at Karachi were kind enough to let it go. The flight took off at 5.30 p.m., September 6, 1958. I had perhaps a couple of hundred dollars in travelers' checks with me. From London, I was scheduled to take the BOAC flight to New York.

1. Reaching the USA

I reached New York's Idlewild International Airport on the morning of September 9th. And from that point onward, I took the cheapest travel possible—the Greyhound bus to my eventual destination, Pullman, Washington. That mode of travel also enabled me to spend nights in bus travel, so I would not have to stay in a motel or hotel. But first I had planned to visit my good friends in Washington, D.C. This is how my diary recounts my experiences during these few days:

September 7th—reached London at local time 2.30 p.m., via Tehran, Damascus, Rome, Geneva. A friend met me at the airport; had a lovely time seeing places with him. Stayed at White Park Hotel for the night.

September 8th—Left London for New York, 9.30 p.m., via BOAC. Here I encountered the excess weight problem that the PIA had let go at Karachi and had to pay about 30 English pounds (about U.S.$60 at the time)—a huge penalty to pay out of my meager resources! Discarding my treasured books was not an option.

September 9th—Reached New York safe and sound—very pleasant journey. Went to American Express; then to Greyhound Bus Office—get ticket for Pullman via Washington, D.C.

Leave for D.C., reached D.C., 10.30 p.m. Went to YMCA, stayed there overnight.

Some interesting experiences happened at the New York airport, before leaving for D.C. At the airport, I needed to go to the bathroom. When asked someone, I was directed to a 'restroom.' But, I asked, I didn't want to rest! So I discovered the bathroom. Then, as I approached the rest-room, I found the door won't open. Again, I learnt my lesson; I discovered that I had to insert a dime to open the door and use the restroom.

Then I needed a porter to get to the taxicab to go to the Greyhound Bus Depot. The Afro-American porter was very pleasant and helpful. Upon reaching the taxicab, I wanted to give him a tip. I took out all the change in my pocket, perhaps about a dollar or so, and I assumed that he would take a quarter or so. But he took the entire change from my hand. Obviously, I couldn't ask for anything back. To my shock, I was thinking of my meager resources—some used for the bathroom and then for the porter.

But now I was in Washington, D.C., September 10th.

And my main reason to come here was to visit my gracious American friends, whose recommendations were critical for my admission. I visited them in their offices. They met me with profuse warmth. They took me around to show me various national monuments. They took me out for lunch and then left me at the Greyhound Bus Depot for my long journey to Pullman, Washington.

2. Greyhound to Pullman, Washington

It was September 10th and the departure time for the bus was a few hours away. I decided to sit in a nearby park and wait. And here was a rather unusual encounter.

As I sat at a bench, dressed in my striped, navy-blue suit and necktie, with my suitcase and briefcase beside me, a limping black man slowly approached me. I was a bit apprehensive. "Hey, would you like to have a girl—blonde, brunette, black, white?" Shocked at his suggestion, I politely responded in the negative. He walked away, only to re-appear a few minutes later. "Hey, would you like to have a beer?" Again, I declined the gesture. He seemed a bit annoyed but walked away. Then, a few minutes later, he again limped toward me, and now asked if I had a cigarette for him. I said, "I am sorry I do not smoke." That did it. He seemed upset and yelled, "What the hell do you do for fun anyway? No girl, no drink, no cigarettes!" That's when I became a little scared. It was quite an exposure to the ugly side of the new world's culture. As he turned around, I quickly picked up my belongings and decided to go and sit inside the security of the bus depot and wait there for the departure time.

Beginning, September 10th, the next few days—and nights—were in bus travel, about 3,000 miles to cover before I would reach Pullman, Washington. The notes in my diary suggest it was a rather excruciating experience. But it was the cheapest mode, I knew. September 12th, "All day in Greyhound bus; bus travel not enjoyable at all; have been able to see places, but feel very lonely." September 13th, "Whole day in bus again! Almost killing me."

But I met some interesting people along the way. I remember at Chicago, a Black- American man in military uniform sat next to me, and we struck a conversation. There was some mutual curiosity. He found that I was to be a foreign student in the country. He asked if I was married; I said, "no…I had other goals to pursue first." I asked if he was married; "no, I am not." Then the conversation drifted into other topics. Then, suddenly, he took his wallet out and showed me the picture of a child. I asked who was the child? His answer, "that is my son." I was shocked; and I reacted, "But you told me you were not married?" His answer, "Oh, well." That was in 1958, when such an inverse sequence of marriage and children was most unusual anywhere and viewed as morally reprehensible. However, now the age-old sequence is often irrelevant—and the reverse is almost normalized.

3. New Home: Pullman, Washington

After four days and nights, finally I reached my destination: Pullman, Washington, the home of the Washington State College, where I would soon begin my new life as a freshman student. Here is my diary again:

September 14th—Reached College Campus Pullman at long last. I was received without difficulty—was taken direct to student convocation. Met the very welcoming foreign student advisor. Felt most miserably home sick, never before in life—don't know what's happening to mind. Feel like going back home. Met some other Pakistanis.

September 15th—Went to see Foreign Student Advisor, a very nice lady. Spent day in college routine. Wrote to mother; met some more Pakistanis; feel better outside, but when alone, feel terrible—just don't know whether I have made a mistake, or I should go back."

September 16th—Again spent day in routines. The foreign student advisor took me out for lunch yesterday, today too. So nice of her. Met some academic advisors. All very encouraging.

September 17th—Quite busy day—met advisors re my major (Business Administration). Chose courses, some of which are advanced. Had a thorough tough physical exam. Reception in the evening at President's house for foreign students; enjoyed it. We all had to introduce ourselves.

September 18th—All day spent in registration formalities. A nice "at home" gathering by Pakistanis in the evening."

September 19th—Picnic with many other foreign students, several miles outside Pullman—good.

September 20th—Saw SCW-Stanford football match. Went to North House. Match won by SCW. Surrounded by colorful ceremonies—enjoyable." (Nothing on 2lst).

September 22nd—Classes begin—student again! Classes rather tough (Courses taken:

Development P.E., Fundamentals (Microeconomics), American Government; English for Foreign Students; and Principles of Accounting; I passed these courses with all B's, except C in Econ.202; being my first semester, almost a B average was a huge relief. Note: went to classes in a suite and necktie (habit from Karachi's job environment); felt absolutely foolish. Soon I was reminded—when in Rome, do as Romans do; soon I was typically wearing blue-jeans, ordinary shirt and jacket. At the time, jeans were viewed as ordinary, cheap wear.

September 23rd—Busy all day in classes

September 24th & 25th—I feel sorry sometime that I should not have come as undergraduate—its rather tough but I shall do my best to succeed now.

September 26th—Life being regularized little bit—attended a Cosmopolitan Club meeting (This was an international students club that met every Friday evening, with some sort of internationally-oriented variety programs).

September 27th—Went to see some Pakistani friends

September 28th (Sunday)—Went to Garry's Church—similar to a mosque! Went South House and North House afternoon" (that's where some other Pakistani and other foreign students lived).

Garry here is, of course, Garry Ratliff, who was one of my roommates at the Stimson Hall, where I stayed. His has been a lifelong friendship. My diary tells me, "On October 9th, I received a package of cookies from Garry's mother—what a surprise! Nice, though!!" I had not even met Garry's parents yet. More on these wonderful links later.

4. Transition to Normalcy

Gradually I was adapting to my new environment and feeling a bit normal concerning my new life and my future challenges. My diary during the second-third weeks of October tells me this: "Nothing particular—days passing in studies—hard work!" "Getting used to college atmosphere." "Nothing unusual—passing days in better spirits." "Gradually, I am developing a liking for my new way of life—studying most of the time, doing my best." "All well—seem to be adjusting better to this place."

During the first few weeks, I met several Pakistani students, mostly graduate students, who attended Washington

State University as part of the U.S.-Aid exchange program, mostly from Faisalabad Agricultural University. There were several Pakistani students, and, of course, their presence was a huge source of comfort for me. Aside from four of us (undergraduates) who were "on our own," all other Pakistani students (about 15 of them) were on U.S. government scholarships. I was the only one strictly on my own, with no financing coming from Pakistan. While some of these friends have passed away, I have continued to be in touch with others with whom I share fond memories. There are so many of them, and at the time, so many of them provided me friendship and moral support during my days of struggles.

I still have in my possession the historic bundle of letters from my mother, my sisters, my dear friends and even their families—all consoling and comforting me, encouraging me in every way possible to somehow learn to survive and not feel lonely and homesick, now that I have sacrificed so much to get here. There were letters full of tears, even moisture imprints from tears showing on the letters, from my sister and my mother—comforting me, yet also lovingly telling me that I should not have done what I did, but now, I must somehow learn to survive—so full of prayers and good wishes for my successes. And missing me terribly—and praying for the day when I would see them all again. Also, many comforting, encouraging letters from close friends, and even their families.

But there were also times, during these early weeks and months that I would just spontaneously start crying while trying to go to sleep. What I am doing here? Why did I let go of a fairly comfortable life in Karachi, with good earnings, good friends, etc.? There was no turning back, however—no way that could happen even if I wanted to;

I came with only one-way ticket. Besides, I often thought of a friend who had come to the U.S. previous year as a student and he felt so homesick that he decided to return—and he did. And then he was miserable for having done so. Knowledge of that story was a strong deterrent.

And in retrospect, there are no regrets whatsoever. It was a hugely rocky road, but my destiny called and eventually reaching my destination has been supremely satisfying.

5. Dormitory Living

Obviously, as a new foreign student, even despite my meager resources, my option at this time was to live in a dormitory; I knew no one else with whom to share an apartment. Besides, most Pakistanis were older and graduate students and well-funded with fairly large scholarships through the U.S. Aid program. So I chose to move into a dormitory; obviously, I had to borrow some money. Dormitory living was a tremendous experience.

I was placed in the Stimson Hall, with two room-mates: Garry Lee Ratliff was one of them—and we have always been in touch. I found Garry to be particularly friendly and sincere; besides, I soon discovered, he and I shared so many common moral values—good old Christian and Islamic values of so many do's and don'ts of life. There were two separate rooms, with a common room in the middle. Garry being a senior had his own room, but I shared the other room with a roommate, with bunk-beds to sleep on. I tried the upper bed, but perhaps was uncomfortable, so my roommate agreed to let me switch to the lower bed. Both were fine room-mates.

Of course, there was a lot of cultural interchange and curiosity. I was the foreign student, from an "exotic" part of the world of which the local students hardly had any knowledge. And this was 1958! Where is Pakistan? Where is India? Oh, is Pakistan part of India? Do they have electricity there? Do they have ice-cream? Various and sundry, but somewhat silly, though understandable, questions. I honestly felt I was more knowledgeable about the world than my American peers.

Living in the Stimson Hall was quite an experience, most rewarding in so many ways. I sort of believed that I should extend myself and try to make an acquaintance or friendship about once daily! Why not?! And there were so many friendships, some that survived the test of time—and I am still connected with some friends, Garry Ratliff stands out the most durable friend; another is Pete Benville, who now lives in California. So many of us from the dorm used to go to eat together in the dining hall—wonderful companionship. Like my peers, I would often go to the library in the evenings to study, for there were quiet hours there. The dorm too had quiet hours on each floor, but not the sort of isolated study environment that the library provided. Sometimes I would study in the dorm room. And we usually had break-times for 10-15 minutes—and our common room often became the draw for others on our floor.

Among my early cross-cultural experiences, one stands out quite distinctly. Someone on our dormitory floor had contracted lice in his hair and perhaps body, so the doctor had asked him to shave off his hair and wear minimum of clothing whenever he could. Now here was the shocker for me. This fellow used to walk around naked on our floor, and during our study-break and other times in the evening, he would just come and sit with us in our room—stark naked!! I could never adjust to it, but it was amusing, however.

And then there were other surprises. We had bathrooms

on the floor with two-three showerheads, i.e., so students could take joint showers if we had to. A huge problem for me, but whenever possible, I used to look for opportunities so I could shower alone, or sometimes I would pick a time when someone else was least likely to join. It didn't always work, however. The same was true in the university gymnasium where I had to accept joint shower situations from the very first semester when I was enrolled in a physical education class and later, in the swimming class during spring 1959; yes, I had to take swimming, for I didn't know swimming; it was a requirement. At the time, four semesters of physical education courses were required; I got used to my joint-shower experiences.

And my friends knew I had never seen snow before, and I was anxious for the sight.

It so happened that once it snowed at night and my roommates made sure that my first exposure to snow would be in my bed while sleeping. They stuffed some snow underneath my blanket! What a surprise, what a joy! I woke up and saw the snowfall through our window for the first time; I was glad from the sights. Of course, I have seen plenty of snow by now—and, any longer, not too terribly fond of it.

A brief note on my acculturation to the new landscape of my life. As the university life progressed, I was quite comfortable with my new life. My academic work, while demanding, was reasonably successful in terms of grades, etc. Given my skills in typing and shorthand, I would always type my own term-papers, etc., and even take classroom lecture notes in short-hand, which, of course, I would translate into English the same evening or soon after.

Obviously, being on student visa, success was most critical; otherwise, there was always the risk of being deported. That would have been an horrible option for me, with none to support my return-trip and none to take me back! So academic success especially during the first couple of semesters seemed rather critical, for initial good performance becomes the base that is often critical to establishing one's credibility and future potential. My personal maturity, determination, and previous work experiences enabled me to relate well with my instructors and I was able to cultivate rather sincere and meaningful links with them. Thanks Almighty, things worked out and I survived just fine. Once the routine developed, the successive semesters, while always challenging, especially combined with the pressures of economic survival, worked out just fine.

6. Linking with Ratliffs

And, as my friendship with Garry Ratliff progressed, he invited me to accompany him to his home during Christmas break, 1958. The Ratliff family lived in a small town, about 150 miles away, called Electric City, Washington, near the Coulee Dam, one of the largest in the country. Garry's father worked at the Dam and his mother worked at the local post office. The visit was most wonderful, the beginning of a life-long, most affectionate relationship. The Ratliffs took me in as their own; they were like my surrogate parents. I visited the Coulee Dam and learned much.

Nearby there was a reservation where indigenous people (native-Americans, or "red-Indians," as they were called then) lived. And, of course, I had seen some Hollywood movies that revolved around battles with the "red-Indians," and I was curious to see them in person.

The Ratliffs took me to a nearby tavern where the "natives" often mingled. I was glad to see them in person.

Some of them seemed inebriated. Noticing some affinity with my complexion, one or two of them approached me to shake hands and talk with me. However, I was cautioned to stay away, for they were "bad" people. That's how I too had perceived them from those movies. However, that stereotyped imagery and my behavior have bothered me ever since.

7. Socialization, Dating

And I was fortunate to cultivate warm friendships with many, Pakistanis and Americans; and many of those links continue till this day. Living in the dormitory also provided opportunities for socialization with the opposite sex, but I had other priorities—academics and survival. And, there were often weekend exchanges between men and women's dormitories, where there would be opportunities for interactions with students of the opposite sex. Of course, there were other opportunities in campus life.

Basically shy, and also constrained by the limits of my own cultural values, I was not much of a mixer. For a long time, I never even thought of going on a 'date.' Then, there was an occasional remark from dorm friends, "What's wrong with you? Aren't you a man?" What a blow to any young man's ego! Yet, I resisted and resisted. Garry Ratliff would also get after me on occasion, but he understood my self-imposed constraints. OK, OK. Then there was this girl who worked at the dining hall—always smiling, always so pleasant. Garry arranged for me a blind date with her. I met her one evening in the CUB (Student Union Building) for a cup of coffee or cold drink. She was already engaged; and that was about it.

Beyond that, during my undergraduate years, I dated occasionally, but I wasn't much of a socializer in this respect;

and I always subjected myself to the culturally-embedded limitations. There was another Pakistani friend. He was the playboy type; often flunking from school and then getting re-instated. Yes, he was well off financially—a regular remittance from back home. He did graduate from WSU, though; it took him a bit longer to finish the undergraduate.

For me, however, there were other challenges—other than surrendering to temptations of a "fun" life. How about my finances? How am I going to survive?

Chapter VII

SURVIVAL STRUGGLES, GRADUATION: 1958–62

As I began my undergraduate education, my limited finances, of course, presented a huge challenge. From what little I had, I paid a small installment for room-and-board, bought the books, bought some very basic life amenities. I had thought I would manage with clothes brought with me, but the very first day I found that going to classes in a suit-necktie just won't fit. Soon I bought a pair of jeans, one or two cheap shirts, and a reversible jacket that would protect me against winter and rain. I also had my long heavy coat with me that I had brought used; that was handy on occasion. But, I remember those jeans and the jacket—I survived wearing them almost the entire four years of my undergraduate years.

1. Part-Time Campus Jobs

How will I survive in the days, months, and years ahead? Usually, the U.S. Immigration Office would not allow a foreign student to take part-time work during the first year. However, I pleaded with the Foreign Student Office for obtaining me such permission; fortunately, it came through and I was allowed to work part-time, 20-hours per week, effective Spring semester. My previous work experience and maturity—and my determination to succeed—were helpful, but not initially. However, I remember, in anticipation of the permission, late during the first semester, I was somehow able to find part-time work in the dining hall where we used to go for our daily meals. My work involved washing dishes, cleaning floors and tables, cleaning bathrooms, etc. Quite a contrast, I used to wonder, to my prestigious supervisory position in Pakistan with U.S. AID office. My academic goals and determination, however, enabled me to accept the situation; I knew it was transitional and I could see light at the end of the tunnel, eventually. Sometimes the work was in the evenings, sometimes mornings. And sometimes weekends. I preferred weekends, because that gave me greater flexibility for my studying priorities.

This job didn't quite provide me the full 20 hours allowed, so I searched for more work. I do recall, once I found part-time work, I learned to be much better organized in the allocation of my time in pursuit of my priorities. There was hardly any time for any diversions. The meager amount of earnings provided some measure of security. And, early on, I also used to get letters from the "step-father" in Lahore to send some money, even though I was literally starving here.

As I searched, another part-time job that became available was in the campus facilities where animals and poultry were kept for research. The job required cleaning the animal-poultry pens; there was always an awful stink, but that was no barrier. Once, I remember, it rained heavily and those pens were flooded, with water accumulated about knee high. And not only the facilities needed to be cleaned, but also the dead turkeys and animals had to be removed. My boss told me about the assignment, and the good thing was that he took the lead. Both of us wore rubber goulashes that went up to our waist and we together cleaned the animal shelters—turkey pens and pig pens. Quite a memorable experience.

Also, occasionally, the boss would ask me to learn to weld some broken tools—and I learnt to do that. The boss was a good person; he appreciated my willingness to do whatever task I was asked to perform; I was hungry. After all, I had learned long ago, during my work experiences in Pakistan, that part of one's success in any endeavor depends upon adopting a "can-do" attitude—and demonstrate a genuine willingness to learn whatever the task. Those were also the demands of survival now, obviously.

2. My Fortunate Encounters

During the first semester, a most wonderful thing happened. I met late Dr. Mark Buchanan, the Director of University's Agricultural Experiment Stations, with whom I had become acquainted in Pakistan in connection with my admission prospects, and he was WSU Exchange-Program's Party Chief there. He was kind enough to give me a part-time clerical job in his office during the Christmas break. My immediate supervisor was a very noble man, Mr. Leonard Young. Both appreciated my work ethic and determination. Both were familiar with my substantial administrative experience from various jobs in Pakistan. Dr. Buchanan was kind enough to circulate a note to the entire campus community, noting my maturity and my skills, and my availability for part-time work. That gracious gesture opened a life-changing door for me. I was contacted by a faculty-member, Dr. Edna Douglas, to see if I would work part-time for her. And that connection turned out to be such a noble, lifelong anchor for me—even after I became a well-established professional in my own right. My deep respect and affection—and gratitude—for her will always be alive.

As a consumer-economics faculty, Dr. Douglas was affiliated with WSU's School of Home Economics. She offered me a part-time job, doing desk-jobs for her—some library research, statistical calculations (yes, manually, or using those noisy Olivetti or Frieden calculators), typing, taking short-hand notes and transcribing, typing manuscripts that she had dictated on the Dictaphone machine tapes, etc. Among other things, she was writing a book and my work related to topics that would be incorporated in that book. I loved the job, for it was a great learning experience, it employed my office skills, and the boss was one of the most remarkable and gracious human-beings I ever encountered in my life—and so compassionate, so appreciative of my struggles to attain higher education under difficult circumstances. I continued to work part-time for her throughout the rest of my undergraduate semesters—and beyond. I was often in touch with her, until her passing away in July 2014. While this job provided me about 10 hours weekly, I continued to work additional hours on the other part-time jobs (dining hall, animal/poultry facilities), totaling the permissible 20-hours per week.

And then there was the link with Professor Theodore R. Saldin, a professor of accounting in the College of Economics and Business. Once he learnt of my background, he took me under his wing. He gave me a part-time office job; and he occasionally invited me to his home.

And then there was another connection—Dr. and Mrs. John A. Guthrie, both deceased now. He was the Director of WSU's Bureau of Economics and Business Research and also Professor of Economics. I met him casually—perhaps through the Saldins, for the two families lived close to each other. Soon, I would occasionally be in the company of the two families, in the home of one or the other. They had a genuine affectionate feeling for me; and they appreciated my determination to succeed—and whatever personal character they observed in me. I also occasionally worked part-time in Dr. Guthrie's Bureau, part-time as well as one or two summers.

Something very special I must note about Jack Guthrie at this time. When I returned to Pullman with my lovely bride, Rukhsana, in the fall of 1965, she wanted to resume her education at WSU. As noted later in this narrative, Dr. Guthrie's assistance was most helpful in that transition.

Another kind person I must mention was a local medical doctor, Dr. Claude Weitz who, knowing my hardships, often provided me medical treatment free of charge.

I shall always be grateful for these encounters in my life.

3. Summer Jobs

Of course, I had learnt, before coming to the USA, that one of the ways many students finance their education is to "work their way through college"—part-time campus work and full-time summer jobs. I had relied on that possibility for my economic survival. But how? Where?

One of my good friends during the first semester was late Bruce Peterson; he died of stomach cancer in 1974. I learnt that his parents, Lawrence and Edith Peterson, owned a fruit ranch in Grandview, Washington (near Yakima Valley). I asked Bruce if his parents would give me some manual job at their ranch for the summer. He talked to his parents and they seemed accommodative. During spring 1959 perhaps, I went with Bruce to spend a few days at his parents' home; both such wonderful people with whom I kept close links as long as they lived. I was the foreign student, from a remote part of the world, an 'international' novelty in the small community. I met some friends of the Peterson family, who welcomed me. Lawrence Peterson was most helpful. He told me that I could work at the ranch during summer 1959. What a huge relief! I could earn some money for my succeeding year.

Of course, I occasionally had to send money to mother secretly—things were extremely dire for her and the family, in addition to what I used to send directly to the "step-father." Looking back at some of the old letters, I find that once, while I am starving here, the monster would want me to send him gifts; once he asked me to send him a BB gun! And, there would be a suggestion occasionally that I should finance the marriage expenses of his daughter, my half-sister, whenever that would take place.

What were my summer job experiences? Retrospectively, wonderful, wonderful—yet at the time, quite a struggle.

4. 1959 Summer: Fruit Orchards

Grateful to the Petersons, my first summer job was at the Peterson Fruit Orchards, Grandview, Washington. Bruce Peterson and I rented a small trailer in which we both lived at the ranch. During the weekdays, his mother would bring lunch for the family, including me, and we will all eat together—such a noble gesture on their part. Bruce and I spent the weekends at the family home. For someone recently arrived in the land, it was interesting to observe the family living style. In the evenings, I would see Lawrence sitting on the recliner chair, watching TV and enjoying his beer. Some time they would go to a local tavern and I would go with them just to observe the scenery. Once Lawrence would be a bit high, there would be arguments between husband and wife—often ending with loving expressions; Edith would often say, "I am the southern belle from Mississippi." Lawrence's roots were from Sweden (and Bruce often feigned a Swedish accent!). Bruce was very averse to liquor, and so was I, of course. Those were the weekends, but weekdays were hard work for everyone, including Lawrence, the ranch owner.

The first several weeks of the summer usually represent the growing/ripening period for any fruit ranch. During this period, there weren't too many workers—there was myself and another individual named Emmett (who would often entice me to accompany him to visit 'fun girls' in a nearby town!). The Peterson ranch was about 100 acres or so, segmented into areas for apples, peaches, and apricots. During the early weeks, my job was to simply walk up and down all day to regulate water flow along the irrigation channels or ditches, with fruit trees on both sides. There was a water tap at the top end of each ditch and the water would flow into each tap from a feeder canal. My job was to regulate the water flow so that it would not be too fast or too slow, but enough for the water to gradually flow from the top end to the bottom. Obviously, rapid flow would cause soil erosion and the moisture won't sufficiently seep into the roots of the trees, and if too slow, the moisture won't travel as fast and some trees could remain un-irrigated. I used to walk up and down along each of the ditches, with a shovel on my shoulder and adjust the water flow here and there as needed. Interesting job and I learnt fast.

And there were interesting experiences—some scary ones. Occasionally, I would see a mountain lion (cougar) at a distance and be frightened, for if I was attacked, I could be seriously injured or killed. I would hide myself behind the trees until the lion disappeared; but the fear would haunt me every day. I would talk about these sightings during lunch time; I understood, however, that any risk was small and I should not worry. I survived alright, however. Then there were occasional encounters with rattle snakes, quite common in the dry climate of the valley. Some time, I would just ignore and they would disappear in their holes. Other times I would chase them away with my shovel and push them into their holes. And then once, during lunch time, I was bragging about a rattle snake and how I chased him and tried to kill him. Then I got a scolding from the boss, Lawrence. I must not hurt snakes; they are predators and kill birds and insects which would otherwise harm the fruit on the trees; lesson learned. Of course, from my previous experiences, every snake is poisonous.

Once, while we were all having lunch, everyone was complaining of a terrible odor, which I too could smell. It was a mystery. After finishing our food, I started recounting my earlier encounter with a small white-and-black striped animal; I chased it to its hole with my shovel. The mystery was solved: the animal was a skunk, which, upon being chased and threatened, would spray the most stinking smell on its target. And that was what had landed on my clothes and that was what everyone was smelling. Of course, I had never seen a skunk, nor experienced the skunk stink ever before; it is not a tropical climate animal. Once the story was told, Lawrence asked me to immediately jump into the nearby feeder canal, with clothes on. And I did. It took a while before the stink evaporated and I could sit in company.

Later during the summer, as the fruits matured, it was time to pick the fruits—apples, apricots, and peaches. There were more workers—Mexican fruit-pickers, known as "wetbacks" at the time, apparently "illegals," who somehow managed to enter the country by swimming through bordering rivers, seeking jobs in the Yakima Valley's fruit orchards. As they encountered me, my brownish complexion confused them as though I too was from Mexico; they would start talking to me in Spanish. And I would blabber back in one of my native languages. Soon, it was clear to them that I was not from Mexico; but there was good affinity with some of them. There is now a large population of Mexican-Americans in the country.

Yet there were other experiences of this summer—two that were life-threatening. Once during the summer, several of us young folks—myself, Bruce, and two others decided to go for a mountain-climbing excursion to Mt. Adams, over 12,000 feet high, a 100 or so miles away in the Yakima Valley area. I don't recall what exactly were others wearing in terms of clothes and shoes, but I had my simple clothes, my reversible light-blue jacket, and light tennis shoes. And all of us embarked on the mountain climbing journey. As youngsters, the idea was to get to the peak of the mountain. Of course, as we walked toward the peak, the weather was colder and there were more and more snow-covered areas. But, onward we kept going somehow, despite my tennis shoes. We managed to climb about near the peak. And then there was the downward descent—easy, of course, for it was downhill and we could even slide downward at times in sitting position, with our jackets tied around our hips.

And then there was an almost fatal experience. As I was sliding downhill on a slope, suddenly I found myself unable to stop—and I could see a deep valley ahead of me into which I would probably plunge and die. I desperately struggled to dig my heels into the snow. Thanks Almighty—eventually, not far from the edge of the valley, I was able to dig my heels into a snow-covered boulder and stop my downhill drift;

and then I slowly managed to back off. Ever since I have wondered: what if I had plunged into the valley and died? Who would have known? Who would have missed me?

Then there was another almost near-death experience. As the summer progressed, my job switched from irrigating the trees to helping the Mexican crew in fruit-picking, hauling, etc. And the hauling usually meant stacking the fruit boxes on a flat-bed trailer hooked to a tractor. I was keen to learn to drive the tractor, not quite as challenging as learning to drive a car. I occasionally did drive the tractor, with Lawrence's permission. Once I was driving the tractor downhill, and then, as I approached a sharp right turn, I didn't slow down enough. So, the tractor flipped leftward, but since the clutch came out, soon the tractor came to a stop. And, to save myself, I jumped off the tractor and reflexively, I managed to land a few yards away. I still wonder: what if the tractor had landed on me as I fell off? I might not be alive today.

And there were some other interesting episodes. Once the Petersons decided to go to Seaside, Oregon, for the weekend, and, of course, I went with them. Seaside is a resort town at the edge of the Pacific Ocean. Lawrence, Bruce and I were in swimming trunks; yes, including me—the 120 pounds weakling that I was. Edith was in her one-piece swim-suit, with her skinny legs exposed. And as we were strolling around the beach, a small dog came nearby—and approached one of Edith's legs. Guess what happened? The dog raised his leg and urinated on her leg, as though it was a tree limb! Edith was disgusted, of course, but that was the story for laughs about every time we all got together in later years.

And then there was my frightening encounter with local police. Bruce and I had gone downtown to some club or perhaps visiting some friends. A bit late at night, Bruce was driving his father's red pick-up and I was sitting on the passenger's side. Suddenly, I had the urge to go to the bathroom. Uncontrollable! I asked Bruce to stop somewhere, or else I might mess up the inside of the pickup! He stopped near the local school grounds. I quickly opened the door and ran toward a tree where I could go, and in my hurry to close the door, I injured the back of my hand and there was some blood running. As I was urinating next to a tree, suddenly there was a flood-light flashing on me, and I wondered why anyone would want to focus on me in that condition. Soon, it was clear.

A policeman stopped his car and approached me. Who am I? I am, of course, shaking in fear and anxiety. What will happen now? Arrested? Deported? End of all my ambitious plans? I tried to explain my situation, as did Bruce. He won't believe. And when he saw some blood on my hand, he was sure I was a Mexican wetback who had committed some crime, or I was in a brawl. I explained how the injury had happened and that I was a foreign student at WSU; of course, Bruce also argued my case. But the policeman was reluctant to believe us and was threatening to arrest me and take me to jail; and I was ready to faint. Then Bruce mentioned his father's name and that I was a summer worker at the family ranch. The policeman had me sit in his vehicle, and we all drove to the house. Lawrence explained everything to the policeman—and then only, I was cleared! What a relief, what an experience!

And, as a foreign student, I was a bit of a novelty in this small town. Coming from an exotic land of the East, non-European world, I was the object of curiosity—I mean that quite sincerely. Whenever the Petersons would be invited somewhere, I would also be invited. And Petersons' friends and neighbors, as well as other community folks, would contact me and would want to know more about me, my background, how I came to this country, what was Pakistan all about—the culture, the economic conditions, etc. Hardly anyone seemed to have any familiarity with the non-European world, substantially true even today; it was quite appalling for me then and so it is even today. Once the local newspaper interviewed me and published a story about me. Scanned copy of that interview, dating back to summer 1959, is attached at the end of this discourse. Great summer experience.

5. 1960 Summer: Lumber Mill, Lewiston, Idaho

Academic year 1959-60 passed by, having lived another year in the Stimson Hall, with quite satisfactory grades (Dean's List each semester, which meant B or above grade-average). Life was pretty routine now, my determination stronger than ever, my goals were rather clear—earn my bachelor's degree, and then perhaps go to graduate school, or go back to Pakistan and take a fancy job there, get married, and live happily thereafter. But, meantime, there was the matter of survival here. Of course, there were my part-time campus jobs. But what about summer 1960?

A friend from India, Balbir Singh Sandhu ("Bill" as he was called) mentioned about exploring job prospects with the Potlatch Lumber Mill, Lewiston, Idaho, about 30 miles from Pullman. He had worked at this Mill the summer before, so he suggested, why not both of us try our luck there for summer 1960? It seemed agreeable, for there was no other viable option. Someone drove us to Lewiston and we signed up at the Mill for summer jobs. We rented an apartment, with some basic furnishings, near the Mill (called Millview Apartments), so we would be within walking distance; obviously, we didn't have our own vehicle—neither one of us even knew how to drive! At the apartment, we had to get a telephone, so the Mill personnel office could reach us in case a job prospect arose.

We both would pretty much stay in the apartment most of the time, glued to the telephone, waiting for the call for a job. After a week or two, Bill was called, for he had seniority, having worked there the summer before. I was still waiting, but in another few days or so, I too received the job call. The job paid 90 cents per hour, which was OK for those days, but what a joy, what a relief to have the summer job! Both of us were assigned to the Mill's veneer plant, and we were given the grave-yard shift (11p.m. to 7 a.m.). Trying to get some rest and sleep during the day was a challenge, especially with the noisy traffic of logging trucks all day on the adjacent road.

Our job entailed standing beside the conveyer-belts and picking up and stacking on the side long pieces of sliced veneers that were moving along; it wasn't easy for this 120-pound weakling; there is a picture at the end. Of course, we had to wear heavy gloves, for protection against splinters. It was an all-night job, monotonous and boring, but so what—it was my means of survival. Both of us being foreign students attracted attention from our co-workers, nice, friendly bunch. Bill belonged to India and his Sikh religion required him to wear a turban and grow a beard; obviously, he would draw special attention for that appearance. Once our foreman approached him and asked if he could at least remove his turban for the safety of others. Why? Because, he was told, that others often, out of curiosity, keep looking toward him, and someone might get hurt from the moving conveyer belts. Bill obliged; survival instinct prevailed, and he trimmed his beard and hair, and he took off his turban.

Later, I was assigned to the paper-plant, still the grave-yard shift, where the job required, among other things, helping move giant-sized rolls of paper from one area to another.

We both managed the summer in this environment. There were some friendly neighbors with whom we interacted. We did not have a car, so we would often walk a mile or so to buy our groceries. Sometime, Bill would show his thumb to passing cars for a hitchhike ride—something I have never ever done. Rarely we would get a ride, most often we had to just walk both ways. Then Bill thought of an ingenious approach: Why not put his turban on? Perhaps that would help us get rides, since someone with a turban and beard was a rarity. Sure enough—it worked! Once, as we were walking to the grocery store, Bill showed his thumb for a ride, and a station-wagon stopped. As Bill approached the vehicle, he saw the van occupied with family and children, but the driver offered us the ride. Bill said, "But, sir, there is hardly any room in the car?" The driver answered, "That's OK; get in; we will manage; our kids want to see you!" Bill's exotic appearance was the obvious draw. That approach often enabled us to get rides. Hilarious memories.

And during this summer, not only friends from Pullman would sometimes visit us, but also the Ratliffs from Electric City also came. I remember their neighbors, Happy and Elsie, also came with them; and Alex Gunkel, a campus friend, also accompanied them. I remember we all went to the riverside and enjoyed a picnic meal and enjoyed each other's company. What wonderful memories of the Ratliffs. Their affectionate support for me was always so meaningful and so uplifting.

And now there was the temptation to buy a car. In retrospect, it was a very poor choice. With my meager income, from which also to save for next year's expenses, how do I buy a car? So a close friend suggested joint ownership. Sure enough—we bought a used 1950 Ford Custom car for $150; it was a clutch-system car—automatic transmissions were hardly common at the time. We are now car-owners, though technically it was registered in my name, for the joint-owner, being on a government scholarship, could not own a car. The car would stay with me in Lewiston. Neither one of us, however, knew how to drive! And here is another interesting story of my life.

I studied the driver's license manual, and before too long, I took the written test for the license. I passed the test with something like 98% and before I could schedule a practical driving test, I received the regular driver's license in the mail! Apparently, someone goofed.

But now I have the license to drive, although I don't know how. Also, I could get car insurance, since I had the license. Foolish as I was, I would try to drive the car on my own. Somehow, I would manage to drive, with some struggle. I remember one lesson learnt was when the car would die at a stop sign. I would manage to move again. Finally, once a driver from the car behind me came out to see what was wrong that my car was dying at the stop sign. He yelled at me, "Look, you must keep the clutch pressed down when you stop the car at the stop sign." That's when I understood the function of the clutch! While some friends had explained the functions of the clutch, but I had no practical lessons. Lessons came the hard way.

And now, slowly I started to practice driving on my own. Sometime a friend would give me the lessons. And finally, after having the license for a couple of months, I learnt to drive with some confidence! And I have never, to this day, taken a practical driving test ever! When I moved back to Pullman from Lewiston, I received the Washington license because I had the valid Idaho license; and it was the same story, wherever I went, during all the subsequent years.

Oh, yes, the car we had bought turned out to be a lemon, sold by the proverbial used-car salesman. We discovered it had a cracked block, which meant that it would lose fluid from the radiator frequently and the car engine would heat up. Also, being a used car, it burnt considerable oil. We always kept a gallon of used mobile-oil and also plenty of water for the radiator. Incidentally, later during the fall semester, a friend borrowed the car and it was returned with damaged and jammed pistons! It was junk now. And there was the joint ownership. What do I do? With the help of my then-roommate, however, we took the vehicle to a nearby junk-yard and we installed a used engine and paid about $40.00 for it. And now the car was operational and had some resale value. Before too long, I sold the car for about $100. And I split the amount with the joint owner. Our friendship survived.

Later, of course, I bought some other clunkers. One was an old Chevy which literally used more oil than gasoline, or just about! And those were the days when gasoline cost about 30 cents per gallon and, yes, cheap used oil was available for this oil-guzzler! Another was a Hillman Minx which had very bad front ball-joints, so that the front wheels would almost collapse to one side or the other and to stabilize the vehicle, I had to hold the steering wheel tightly to avoid accidents. And then there was an old Plymouth which ran OK, but once, after I had driven to Electric City to visit the Ratliffs, I found a piston tie-rod had broken, so it had to be repaired there. But the guy who repaired it told me that the car had been running only on four cylinders—somehow the other two were nonfunctional. He advised me to very slowly drive back to Pullman; and I did. Later, I sold that car to someone for $30 or so. Fascinating history of my cars during the undergraduate years.

6. Summers 1961, 1962, and B.Sc. (Honors)

By now, I was quite comfortable with my student life and reasonably confident about my economic survival, given my part-time job with Dr. Edna Douglas particularly. Remarkable lady that she was, she had developed considerable confidence and respect for my skills and my work-ethic. For summer 1961, she offered me a full-time job as her research assistant; of course, I jumped at the opportunity—not only a decent desk job, but also a great learning experience. Obviously, that was quite a step forward, compared to my labor jobs during summers of 1959 and 1960.

But where would I live during these 1961 summer months? I had lived in the dormitory, both during the academic years 1958-1959 and 1959-60, and then roomed with a good friend in a cheap, deteriorated shack during academic 1960-61 and 1961-62 (see picture at the end of this narrative). Incidentally, that shack has its own special stories—e.g., its round-shower was so narrow that while taking a shower, one had to shrink and squeeze a little to avoid touching the cold, plastic surround! And with extremely poor insulation, we used multiple blankets at night and wore sweaters during the day. And, further, since we were both miserably poor, we survived on cheap meals, usually canned spaghetti and beans. I remember there were occasions, not having enough milk, I would manage with a bowl of cereal, mixed in water and sugar; that was good enough as the meal for the day.

As for my 1961 summer living, there was a friend from

the campus Catholic fraternity. And I happened to mention about my summer-living predicament. He suggested that while all students would be gone, I could perhaps live in the empty fraternity and won't to have to pay any rental; my responsibility will be to simply take care of the premises, in particular mow the yard regularly. I will have a choice of beds to sleep on and a kitchen to cook my food. He checked with others in his fraternity and got their clearance. What a break! Excellent. I would reside there for free and do all the chores as a caretaker. In fact, sometimes some other friends also spent nights there; there were plenty of beds to sleep on.

And my lawn-mowing experiences? Nothing spectacular, except that once, while mowing the yard, I saw a snake crawling nearby. And, naturally, I picked up the nearby shovel and wanted to kill it; for me, all snakes were poisonous. However, just as I was about to do the murder, a young lad ran toward me, yelling, "Don't kill, don't kill." And I wondered what was wrong with the lad. And, then the lad reached over and picked up the crawler with his bare hands, as I yelled, "don't, don't." "No, no, it is a grass snake, not dangerous; and I have some more at home; and some scorpions," he answered. And that was that. I felt pretty small and embarrassed. But this is how I discovered that there are non-poisonous snakes in the U.S. Last time I had seen snakes was in the fruit-orchards where I worked during summer 1959—and those were poisonous rattlers. Or, as a youngster, when I used to take "step-father's" goats for grazing.

And now began my senior year—academic year 1961-62—toward graduation, the most cherished milestone of my educational goals thus far. *I earned my bachelor's degree in Business Administration, with honors—and Dean's List during each of the eight semesters!*

It was a magnanimous, yet humbling, feeling, it was ecstasy—something I used to dream about for years, ever since I had finished my 10th-grade matriculation back in 1951. What a struggle during those four years—washing dishes, working as a janitor, cleaning pig-pens and turkey-pens, etc.! But now I was on top of the world. Psychologically such a relief, so relaxed, so joyful. And yet there were moments I wept for the memory of my late father; how proud he would have been to see his only son accomplish this goal. Who is there back home to appreciate what I had accomplished?

Yet the struggle for survival. What about my job for the summer of 1962? I worked part-time for Dr. Douglas and also I had a part-time job with Dr. Guthrie's Bureau of Economic and Business Research. But, oh, what a wonderful summer that was! Having earned the bachelor's degree, and now I was determined to go on for a master's degree in economics and, based on my credible academic record, WSU had granted me admission in the graduate program. And Dr. Douglas had extended me a research assistantship for the duration of my master's program. Suddenly, I could look forward to being "rich:" the assistantship will pay me about $250 per month, a big jump from the monthly $100 or so I used to earn from part-time jobs. No longer the day-to-day anxiety of survival.

During summer 1962, I also decided to reward myself: do some traveling and see the beautiful sights of America. Before that, however, a special tribute to some very special folks is appropriate: the Saldins and the Ratliffs. They were always my moral support and source of encouragement during my critical undergraduate years. Also, during late spring 1962, I discovered a close relative who was a graduate student at WSU for the previous 2-years; we decided to travel together later in summer 1962.

Chapter VIII

MY ANCHORS;
MY TRAVELS

There is hardly any mission that a human-being pursues and accomplishes alone. While one may be the singular driving force, there are always others along the way who, in whatever minor or major ways, often provide critical support toward achieving success. There were numerous gracious individuals who assisted me at various stages of my arduous journey as well as provided inspiration in achieving my early academic goals. Previously, I have talked about my encounters—Dr. Buchanan, the Ratliffs, Dr. Douglas, the Saldin family, the Guthries family. Each played hugely crucial roles, directly or indirectly, as my most helpful mentors and friends for my economic survival during the undergraduate years. Indeed, they were my constant sources of inspiration and encouragement, so critical to achieving success in my academic life. However, the Saldin and the Ratliff families stand out uniquely in my journey.

1. The Saldins

How did the Saldins link arose? I met Professor Theodore Saldin perhaps in 1959 or 1960; and the initial common thread was the fact that he and his family had spent two years in Pakistan, as part of WSU's Exchange Program. Another angel of a human being in my life, soft-hearted, most gentle in his demeanor, filled with compassion and understanding for others—and so appreciative of what I was trying to accomplish in my life.

And my links with the Saldin family became a lifelong treasure, and the nostalgia overwhelms me. Professor Saldin also gave me a part-time job, helping him in some grading, recording, typing letters, etc. Sometimes I felt as though he just "created" some hours of work to help me out. Now I had enough hours from office-type jobs and didn't need the manual jobs that I did during the first few semesters. Of course, I had to keep in focus my primary goal. Flexibility in my part-time work hours allowed me to concentrate on academic work, for success in that respect, with decent grades, was the supreme objective. After the bachelor's degree, I was now determined to proceed to graduate studies for master's and doctorate work.

The Saldins link was one of the most joyful links—and, I am grateful that my family also reciprocated similarly. Aside from my student life, they were also so much a part of our married life, as well as the lives of our children. Throughout those years, the Saldins always connected and we often visited each other for dinners or just to spend a pleasant evening. Jean often made some hand-crafted gifts for our children. Of course, Jean took care of our new-born daughter when Rukhsana had to participate in her graduation ceremonies.

Uniquely remarkable, gracious lady that she was, Jean Saldin passed away in 2000. The tragic event happened at home and I was so touched that I was the first individual Ted called to convey the sad news and I immediately rushed. Their love for each other was always so obvious. I had never seen Ted in such grief before and I comforted him as best as I could, with Jean's body lying on a stretcher nearby. In the following years, we tried to make sure that we connected with Ted as often as possible; we knew he was always so comfortable and relaxed in our company—and with our children. Ted Saldin passed away in 2014. They were such an integral part of our lives; and we continue to miss them very much. We are occasionally connected with their children.

2. The Ratliffs

My friendship with Garry Ratliff began when we met during the first few days after my arrival at Washington State University; he was my roommate in the Stimson Hall. This link developed into a lifelong friendship. As Thanksgiving holidays approached, he invited me to accompany him to his home in Electric City, near Coulee Dam, Washington, about 150 miles away. Garry had his 1946 Plymouth car. His parents, Willene and Luther Ratliff, took me in with so much warmth and love; I was about like a second son for them, and Garry like a brother; and I took them about like my American 'parents." And that's how this fond relationship began—and matured. They would write letters of encouragement to me or call me on the phone. They even wrote letters to my mother and my elder sister in Pakistan, to assure them that I was OK. I remember my mother and sister also wrote back and conveyed their gratitude.

The Ratliffs were always there for me; they extended moral support, affection, and encouragement. They were my anchors who lifted me up and boosted my spirits when the challenges seemed cumbersome. They came to attend the June 1992 graduation convocation and share my moments of glory; Garry could not come—he was away on duty with the U.S. Air-Force. They gave me a wonderful gift, a WSU graduation ring, my cherished possession ever since.

For these American "parents" of mine, even though both have passed away, I always had—and continue to have—so much affection and gratitude. Throughout my younger life, my own 'gaps' always persuaded me to look up to elders who would show some affection. There were my close friends' parents in Pakistan, and now the Ratliffs here. They were my family, my elders, my well-wishers, and friends. Occasional visits to the Ratliffs continued for the next several years.

After Garry had graduated in 1960 and taken a career with the U.S. Air Force, then I would alone go to visit them as opportunities arose, during Thanksgiving or Christmas breaks or during the Spring breaks. They always welcomed me so warmly. There were also occasions when they would come to the campus to visit me, and I would, of course, do my best to extend my hospitality. They would also give me gifts on occasions of Christmas, as I also would reciprocate, despite my meager resources; and they would send me boxes of cookies, as they used to when Garry was on the campus. Luther worked at the Coulee Dam Irrigation Project, which I visited often, and occasionally some Pakistani friends would accompany me and they too would always be welcomed by the Ratliffs and get a tour of the Coulee Dam. The Ratliffs bred and raised beagle dogs, partly as a hobby and as a home business. They were such a loving couple, always expressive of so much love for each other.

During these years, I also met Garry's maternal grandparents, who lived in Spokane. Once when, perhaps during Christmas break of 1960, Garry and I traveled to his home, his grandparents were also there. Such affectionate folks, but rather innocently simple. I remember once, as we were ready to drive back to Pullman, Garry's grandma told him to be sure to hang the St. Christopher icon on the dash-board of the car; that Christian icon is supposed to ensure safety while traveling. Garry told his grandma, "But Grandma, Ghazi is a Muslim." She replied, "That doesn't matter. St. Christopher does not know that!"

And then, from 1962 to 1964, as I was pursuing my master's program, I used to visit the Ratliffs occasionally, and sometimes they would come to Pullman to visit me and meet other friends from Pakistan. This was the routine. And in 1964, as I completed my master's degree, they came again for the convocation ceremonies, just as they did in 1962 for my bachelor's degree. They were truly my family and I adored them enormously for all the affection they showered on me.

During all those years and beyond, I was always in contact with them, even when I moved to Brown University (Rhode Island) in the summer of 1964; while there, they used to send me small, reel-to-reel tapes with supportive, encouraging messages. Given my compulsive habit of saving everything, I have scores of letters from both Mom and Dad, but especially Mom (and of course, from Garry); and I have looked back and read them occasionally, with nostalgic emotions. I don't know how to part with those letters—and so many others from my mother, sisters, relatives and friends (and yes, also, from that monster, the "step-father"), of which I have several sacks! Then, as a married man, I returned to WSU in 1965, with my charming bride, Rukhsana, in order to continue my doctoral program; and, soon after, we both visited the Ratliffs.

And then came a shocker about the Ratliffs. Late 1966 or so, I got a call from Willene—Luther, her husband, had left her for another woman, his high-school sweetheart. I was utterly devastated; I was in tears from the shock, for that was the last thing I could ever imagine about them. The very next day, leaving my lovely wife behind (we got married in 1965), I drove to Electric City, Washington, to see if I could beseech them to reconcile and reunite. I was too optimistic; the split was irreversible; and they divorced soon after. And to this day, I agonize from that shock, for having known them almost since the day of my arrival in the U.S., I had seen them as my ideal of a loving, married couple; the divorce was absolutely unimaginable for me. Yet I remember and miss them, with fondest of memories.

God Almighty has given to His creatures a finite, natural cycle of life; and we are all mortals. The senior Ratliffs are no more. Luther passed away in 1987. After re-marriage, he had moved to Salem, Oregon. Willene also remarried but things didn't work out for her. Later, she moved to Spokane, Washington, to be near her son and his family, for he had taken retirement from the Air Force and was now settled in Spokane, as a school teacher—and since retired from that profession as well. We would often visit her in Spokane; and sometime, Garry, Treva and Mom also would visit us in Moscow, Idaho. But I am getting a bit ahead of the story. Willene passed away on November 11, 2005, at age 89; remarkable lady, fond memories. Of course, Garry and his wife, Treva, continue to live in Spokane and we are regularly in touch.

These few lines about the Ratliffs really do not do justice to my long, affectionate link with them. These fond memories are often relived whenever we visit with Garry Ratliff and his family.

As I age into the twilight zone of life, such nostalgia is my spiritual therapy.

3. Cousin Discovered

It was probably during the spring semester of 1961-62 school year. Several of us friends were sitting in the campus student-union building. And we were talking of an earthquake that had recently happened in Montana. I happened to mention the story of my maternal aunt (my mother's elder sister)—how she and her children perished in an earthquake in Quetta, Pakistan, in 1935, the only survivor being her husband, my uncle. As I shared the story, this friend stood up and embraced me warmly; it turned out that the husband—my uncle—was his paternal uncle, his father's younger brother; we discovered we were cousins, except that we had never met before. Several years my senior, he also knew a bit about some of the earlier calamities of my immediate family. He was pursuing the doctorate in Chemistry and I had just started my master's in Economics.

During that 1962 summer, I was working full-time for Dr. Douglas, earning what at the time was a 'substantial' income, compared to my meager earnings from part-time jobs earlier. Now, having completed the most difficult milestone of my life, i.e., the undergraduate degree, I felt I had a reasonably clear direction for my future and I felt confident about accomplishing my goals.

Before the end of summer 1962, however, I decided to travel and see more of the United States. That 3,000 miles Greyhound bus journey in September 1958 from New York to Pullman was a dreadful memory; I could hardly appreciate and enjoy any sights along the way. And with the financial security from the graduate assistantship, I decided to buy a rather decent, used car; and this old car gave a magnificent sense of luxury!

So, my cousin and I decided to tour the Western U.S. And we embarked on the well-planned, long adventure, late summer 1962.

4.   Travels: See the USA

We drove from Pullman to Portland, Oregon, along the Columbia River, seeing the sight of Oregon's famous Multnomah Falls along the way, then to Portland, Oregon, and then on to Crater National Park, near Bend, Oregon—a most enjoyable sight. Then drove through the California's magnificent Redwood Forests, including the drive through the famous tree, with its huge, drive-through trunk. And we saw the Paul Bunyan recreational spot along the way. And then traveling on California's beautiful coastal highway, we visited the magnificent San Simeon Hearst Castle, with its most ornate Islamic-Spanish architecture.

Then in San Francisco, we visited various sights for the first time—the Golden Gate Bridge, the most-crooked street, Japanese Gardens, China Town, hippie-streets, etc. And while neither of us was too anxious to experience any night-clubs, there was one that I had much heard about— and that aroused our curiosity; it is now extinct, of course. That was San Francisco's then-quite famous night-club ("Pinocchio," as it was named) where all performers were female-impersonators (males dressed as females)—a huge draw at the time. We did go there one evening. And I remember a funny experience here. As we were laughing at the crazy performers, one of them pulled out the rubber-balloon from his brassiere and dumped it on our table—and the balloon squeaked! And, apparently mad at our laughing, he yelled, "Can you guys do this?!"

And then we visited some university campuses in the area—the University of California, Berkeley campus, the Riverside campus, Stanford University campus, etc. Our next destination was Los Angeles. Here we enjoyed visiting the Disneyland and the Universal Studios. And we drove to various parts around Los Angeles—the Hollywood residential area, the Chinese Grauman Theater on Hollywood Boulevard where we saw the footprints of famous Hollywood stars, embossed in concrete slabs.

Then we were on way to San Diego and northern Mexico. In San Diego, the main attraction was the famous Zoo, which we visited and enjoyed very much. Then we went to the border-town of Mexico, Tijuana; we spent part of the day and evening here; we had been alerted about the town being rough—night clubs, drugs, prostitution, etc. Such activities, of course, were big attractions for sailors from the San Diego Naval Base. Just out of curiosity, we went to a bar—and sat there with our soft drinks. And both of us were solicited by bar girls for more nightly fun; and we disappointed the ladies.

But, our big draw for going to Tijuana, Mexico, was the curiosity of watching the bull-fights. And we went to the bull-fight show. We saw the bull-fights—with all the glamour that I had once seen in the Ernest Hemingway movie ("The Sun Also Rises"). The bull being chased and teased by the matador, and finally killed. People were screaming in excitement. However, for us, it was the most brutal sight. Both of us, however, felt sick to our stomachs to see the bloodiest sight of the dead animal. We left after just one "kill."

Short of resources, we often slept in the car, or occasionally stayed with some friends along the way; sometimes we stayed in inexpensive motels just so that we could rest, shower and change One night, while in Tijuana, we found an isolated street and parked the car to get some sleep. We kept the car windows somewhat down because of the hot weather, but then there were mosquitoes to encounter! So, we hung some towels along the windows and somehow tried to survive the night. As the morning approached, we were awakened by a knock; and here was a policeman threatening to arrest us for having violated the local laws; sleeping in the car in that area was forbidden. It was frightening, but we pleaded our ignorance as visiting foreign students. We were forgiven, and we survived.

Next day, we decided to go a bit deeper into Mexico, to a nearby village called Ensanada. Here, we could observe poverty, about like any underdeveloped country. We spent part of the day here, enjoying some hot Mexican food, and, yes, also enjoying the taste of mangoes; at that time, mangoes were an unfamiliar oddity in the U.S. We were now heading back and we decided to re-enter the U.S. via Mexicali, Mexico, into California, and then on to Yuma, Arizona, for our next destination was Las Vegas, and then the Grand Canyon National Park, Arizona.

As we reached the re-entry station in Mexicali, we encountered an unanticipated problem. While we had our passports and I-20 forms that established our identity as foreign students, I didn't have a valid re-entry visa. My cousin's visa status, however, was valid. And there was none at the entry-point who could issue me a visa. And the next day was labor-day holiday, September lst. There was no way we could be allowed to re-enter, not without a fresh visa. What we do? Go and spend another night on the Mexico side of the border—and come back September 2nd?! We did, we had to—no choice.

And then we went on to Las Vegas, Nevada. That was quite an experience—with all the glitter of lights, night-clubs, and whatever else the "sin-city" could offer. Just for the fun of it, we both played the slot-machines and each of us lost a dollar or two. And we spent much of the day just visiting the accessible areas of the night-clubs, just to see what they were all about. We didn't have the inclination, nor, frankly, resources, to go to any shows. And, of course, we also saw the famous Hoover Dam nearby.

From here, we headed toward the major highlight of our trip—the wonder of the world, the Grand Canyon of Arizona. It was the most magnificent sight I ever saw, a visual experience that was far superior and breath-taking compared to what I had only seen in books and magazines. For miles and miles, such multi-colored layers of rock formations in peaks and valleys, so many sights that one can simply watch and absorb for hours and marvel at the grandeur of this natural wonder, as though leisurely carved by God's own hands.

From here, we headed toward Colorado Spring, Colorado, where there were some friends and acquaintances at the Colorado State University. We spent a day or so here, and then our destination was the Yellowstone Park, Wyoming, via the Grand Teton National Forest. Traveling through the Grand Teton Forests was most enjoyable, only to be surpassed by our sights of the Yellowstone National Park. Another superlative, breath-taking wonder of nature— with beautiful, scenic sights, animal life, plants, water falls, naturally-erupting geysers, and, of course, the Old Faithful. As I often say, Grand Canyon and the Yellowstone Park are about the most fascinating natural sights in the United States, each almost as much of a wonder as the Banff National Park, Alberta, Canada. From the Yellowstone Park, we were heading back to Pullman.

In retrospect, I must say that these travels were most enjoyable—rather leisurely, truly enjoyed the wonder that is America. And the experience was an enormous relief, a sort of a self-reward, after the arduous first four years of my life as an undergraduate student.

And now I was ready to pursue the next phase of my life—graduate studies, something I wanted to pursue for reasons a bit different from my earlier academics. That was, initially, to achieve my bachelor's degree in business, and then, I had thought, return to Pakistan and be an executive of some sort in the business world. However, that aspiration evaporated as I discovered myself to be unfit for that world. It was a huge intellectual transformation; my sights now were set at pursuing graduate education in economics. And the goal was to be a professional economist—either in Pakistan or in the U.S., either work in development planning or in the academic world.

Incidentally, my cousin also played a minor role in my marriage to my beloved wife, Rukhsana. While we were roommates, we would sometime talk of this possibility; both of us knew the family. Upon return to Pakistan in 1964, he had conveyed some hints about my inclination to that family. Apparently, the hint also reached my future wife.

And now my pursuit of graduate studies, beginning fall 1962-63.

Chapter IX

GRADUATE STUDIES

With my undergraduate degree achieved, now my sights were set on graduate studies in economics. Having done reasonably well academically as an undergraduate, admission to the master's program was no concern at all. Also, I had a choice of two graduate assistantship offers—a teaching assistantship from the Department of Economics, WSU, and a research assistantship from Dr. Edna Douglas' research program. I had been working as her part-time research assistant for a few semesters and I always found her to be such a gentle, caring mentor. I chose to accept her offer. It was a huge relief that I would no longer be living, literally, hand-to-mouth, or surviving on one-meal a day, as I sometimes did during my undergraduate years. I was rich! And I had so much confidence for a decent future now. I began my graduate studies during fall 1962-63 academic year.

1. Master's Degree

While the course work for the master's was challenging, I found, however, that this challenge was far easier to handle than the undergraduate work. During those earlier years, there was not only a higher load of course-work each semester (and in a variety of fields, some less exciting than others); there were the constant pressures of both academic survival and economic survival. And add to that also the worry about sending a few dollars periodically to my mother and "step-father." For each semester of my master's program, my grades were far superior to my grades during the undergraduate years—almost straight A's during the three-semesters of master's course-work. During spring semester 1963-64, I enrolled to complete the master's thesis.

I chose to do my master's thesis research on Pakistan's economic development. To undertake research at this level was a challenge, but I was anxious to take it. My thesis title was "Financing Investment in Pakistan's Economic Development." I began work on the project during summer 1963. Of course, I would do all the typing myself—why hire someone when I had the skills and could type at a speed of around 60-70 words per minute? I had, of course, acquired that skill as a 15-years old youngster when preparing myself for a job as typist back in those early days of my struggles in Karachi. That skill paid off throughout my academic pursuits and professional career. I typed the various drafts and the final version, to the satisfaction of the graduate school. Obviously, I also used to type all my term-papers, etc. during those years. I successfully defended my thesis project on January 14, 1964. And now, as of spring 1963-64, I had earned a master's degree in Economics.

And, as with other milestones, I remember I missed my late father profusely on that day when I successfully defended my thesis and also on the day in June 1964 when I walked in the WSU convocation procession. How would he feel to see his son achieve this milestone, I wondered? Perhaps he was always watching and keeping an eye on me. And there were, of course, the Ratliffs, my American 'parents,' who came to attend the graduation ceremonies, as they had done for my bachelor's degree convocation. To acknowledge once again, their moral support was always so meaningful for me.

2. Plans for Doctorate

As I was approaching the completion of master's, I also initiated plans to pursue the doctorate in economics. In order to seek admission and financial assistance at various graduate schools, I had to take the Graduate Record Examinations, both general aptitude and in the chosen field of economics. I did—and I remember I scored in the top 99th percentile in both. That enabled me to obtain admission in some of the top universities in the country, including the ivy-league's Brown University, Providence, Rhode Island; and that University also awarded me a full fellowship for the doctorate program. I chose to attend this University during fall 1964-65.

At the end of summer 1964, I planned to move to Providence, Rhode Island.

During all these years, by now six years, I often missed my mother, sisters, and close friends in Pakistan, whose expressions of love and affection through letters were always my emotional source of survival. Now that I have accomplished my bachelor's and master's degrees, I yearned to somehow visit Pakistan to see my loved ones. During those days, about the only contact was through periodic letters; phone calls almost impossible—prohibitively expensive and, besides, no home phones on the other end. I was desperate to go home to Pakistan, but never had adequate resources to go; a roundtrip to Pakistan required a sizeable sum of money. I must still wait a bit longer; perhaps after I have initiated my studies at Brown, perhaps even beyond.

3. Travel East: Brown University

The more immediate concern, however, was how do I travel to the east coast, with all my accumulation of books and personal effects? My own car won't make it, so I had sold it. Fortunately, I found a WSU faculty member who wanted his station-wagon automobile driven to the east-cost. Perfect. I loaded up all my belongings in this car and headed East late August 1964 to join Brown University. This was a leisurely trip, and along the way, I was able to see some wonderful sights of the United States. During the 7-8 days of travel, I sometimes slept in the car, sometimes stayed with friends along the way, and occasionally spent a night in a cheap motel.

As I reached Providence, Rhode Island, I met a good friend, whom I knew well from his days at WSU and who had since moved to Brown on a post-doctoral position in Physics. Always a thorough gentleman, I stayed with him a few days till I arranged my own living quarters. Before the semester started, I also connected with some other friends, as previously planned. These friends had been traveling from the West coast earlier and joined me in Providence. And then, in their car, we leisurely drove to Canada, via north-eastern USA, on way to Toronto, Montreal, and Quebec. Those were most memorable few days of sightseeing and pleasant time with good friends.

Upon return from these travels, I began my graduate studies at Brown University. It was a new environment, not just academically but socially and geographically as well. While the departmental faculty was helpful and friendly, however, I felt that my connections didn't quite have the same warmth and approachability as it used to be at the Washington State University. Of course, Brown had awarded me a fellowship that covered all expenses (except books and supplies, of course). I was determined to succeed. I was able to make my living arrangements with two other graduate students from the Economics Department, one from Sweden and another from Tunisia. It wasn't the best arrangement, but workable. Each of us lived quite independently, without a great deal of cordiality; it was about like a dormitory. We did our own cooking, or often ate outside. Soon, I also bought a used car—I remember it was a 1954 Chevrolet.

4. Health Issues, Changing Course

I successfully completed the fall semester, and then enrolled for some courses during the spring semester. And now I experienced a rather serious health problem. I was told by the hospital doctor I was suffering from a nervous breakdown. Why? When I look back, I can think of several factors, perhaps the most important being the emotional stress of not having seen my loved ones in Pakistan for almost seven years. What was perhaps dormant for some years became alive and painful. Also, the new environment was not all that congenial for my emotional well-being, and I did miss the comfortable life of Pullman, Washington, where I had spent six most significant years of my life. There was also the stress of academically succeeding in a new environment, with high expectations.

And, then there was also this: the sense of loneliness, despite being not alone. Who can I relate to? Who is a genuine, sincere friend, confidant? There was a growing sense that here I am—28 years old, yet none to call my own, as a life partner. I always told myself and others that there comes a time in every human being's life when, aside from the biology of life, there is the psychological need for belonging to another of the opposite sex. It is indeed natural. I was at that stage of life, I felt. I was ready to belong to someone and share my life in marriage——someone with mutual love, care, and sense of belonging.

This was during the spring semester, 1964-65. As my emotional condition worsened, it became difficult to concentrate on studies. The Department extended understanding for my situation and they allowed me to drop the courses in the hope that I would overcome my health issues and then resume studies in the fall of 1966-67. However, my condition worsened, and I was hospitalized for a few days at the University hospital.

So, as the semester progressed, I went through considerable soul-searching, and after conversations with some good friends, I made two major decisions. First, I decided that somehow I must visit Pakistan and re-connect with my loved ones there. How? Well, I will try to save enough, or even borrow, for a roundtrip air-ticket via some group-chartered flights that at the time were often available for the Indo-Pakistan continent. In addition to my fellowship resources, I also found a part-time manual job on the campus to supplement my finances; yes, I was quite accustomed to manual jobs from elsewhere. Second, I decided to return to WSU and resume my doctoral program there, effective fall 1965-66. Frankly, I did miss considerably all my associations in that area, and during this semester, I re-established contact with various mentors there. While they were surprised at my decision, they expressed enthusiastic willingness to have me back in the program. They re-admitted me in the graduate school and offered me a teaching assistantship upon return. I informed the Brown Economics Department; they were disappointed, but they understood.

Before resuming my doctoral program at WSU in the fall of 1965-66, I made plans to visit Pakistan during summer 1965. Financial means were scarce, but I decided to borrow some funds from a good friend. I indicated to my sister and mother that a tentative purpose of my visit was also to get married if a suitable match emerges.

And these events require a separate chapter—my long-overdue return to Pakistan, re-connecting with relatives and friends, and, of course, marriage.

Chapter X

1965: PAKISTAN VISIT AND MARRIAGE

Here it was summer of 1965, at long last, after seven years, I made plans to visit my loved ones in Pakistan. Also, I was thinking of perhaps getting married in Pakistan if a compatible, mutually acceptable match becomes available. During those days, some groups used to arrange relatively inexpensive round-trip, chartered flights for students from New York to Pakistan and India. I had some savings, but I had to borrow some money for the travel. I had all the necessary documents to return to the USA on a student-visa to resume studies at Washington State University, including evidence of a teaching assistantship at WSU.

1. Arriving Karachi

It was early in July 1965 when I left for Pakistan. I remember the flight went first to Bombay, India, and then to Karachi; it was Swissair, I recall. Because of some confusion about flights, I could not inform my sister, or any friends, as to when the flight would arrive Karachi. When it did, I recall, I got off the air-plane and took a taxi to the house where my sister and her family lived and where I too lived before I left for the USA in 1958. As I reached the house, our emotions, pent-up over all these years, exploded—and there was a flood of tears, tears of joy and renewal. Here it was—early July 1965; and I was gone for seven years!

My dearest sister—we hugged and kissed each other warmly; after all, she was about like my mother during those early years and somewhat filled the gap of my deprivations. Her husband also welcomed me warmly. And, of course, there were my nieces and nephews as well—they were all over me with hugs and kisses. I could clearly see, with five children to nurture, and my sister the primary breadwinner, the family was living in difficult economic conditions, just barely surviving. What a great lady that sister of mine has been all her life—such patience, such stamina, such caring, despite all that she herself encountered and endured in her own life.

And soon the word got out and friends came to visit—my dearest friends, Asif and Mushahid, plus some others perhaps. And then I visited their families, so much a part of my earlier years. I found out that Asif's older brother was soon to be married. And I was expected to attend the ceremony. I was also supposed to take color-slide pictures of the occasion with my 35mm camera. At that time, color pictures were a rarity in Pakistan. One could take color pictures, but there were no processing facilities in Pakistan; that had to be done abroad, which is what I had intended to do. I had taken several rolls of 35mm color-slide film. I was anxious to oblige, for I had a great deal of affection and respect for the groom, a gem of a man, who once favored me by facilitating a job back in 1952 and who would also write to me, and even send an occasional gift for me, when he was a Fulbright scholar in the USA in the 1950s. How could I forget?!

However, as I arrived at the ceremony, I recall, in the

excitement of meeting so many from that family and some friends, I hurriedly got off the scooter-rickshaw that took me there, but I forgot my camera in it. That was it. What to do now? Well, Asif's had his own 35mm camera which, with my film rolls, became available for the wedding pictures; and that camera also became available for my use during my stay in Pakistan.

2. Marriage: Some Background

Now during the few days in Karachi, there was conversation with my sister about my own marriage possibility. And she had a few candidates already in mind for me to consider. I appreciated her efforts, but I told her that I also wished to explore possibilities in Lahore. I recall I hinted the possibility of our uncle's daughter—the uncle who played such significant roles in our earlier years. However, that suggestion did not go well with her. She had her reasons, beyond my comprehension even now.

And why that possibility occupied my mind? I need to elaborate and provide some background.

Well, I had known my uncle for a long time and I always felt that he genuinely cared for his sister (my mother) and the rest of us. Of course, he had had his own aches and pains from the disappointments he experienced from his sisters. Further, he did manage to salvage some of our father's resources which became useful for us, including my sister's teacher-training education. And some of those resources also became available for my needs while I was going to school in my foster-homes (Rawalpindi and Karachi). Those aspects of his character were rather admirable. He had faithfully saved those resources, even though our mother often blamed him of misuse and abuse. But, he did not. In fact, his diary contains so many pieces of evidence about his integrity and honesty.

Further, while I was struggling in Pakistan, I often used to get encouraging letters from this uncle, guiding me for a decent career. Soon after my high-school completion, he even encouraged me to come to Lahore, so I could perhaps go to college there, or learn some other job-oriented skills. I did go to Lahore for that objective, but for various reasons, things did not work out. And I returned to Karachi later in 1951.

And after I returned to Karachi, I used to write to him and seek his advice. Of course, I used to yearn for more education, but that was not to be at the time. And whenever I used to go Lahore, between 1952 and 1958, to see my mother, I would always go, accompanied by mother, to see my uncles, but specially this uncle who was sympathetically involved in our calamities during my childhood days. These visits were always rather meaningful, not only in terms of his affection but also the clues I would get about the early history of my own family.

Later, this uncle and his family moved to another town, Kasur, about 40 miles from Lahore. And during my Lahore trips, I would go there as well to see him and the family. Often a bit indifferent to my mother, yet I could also sense the instinctive love of a brother toward his sister. Sometimes he would laugh off her accusations against him, yet I could always sense—and understand— his pains and agonies.

Then, just before departing for the USA in 1958, I went to Lahore to bid farewell to my relatives, especially my mother, uncle and younger sister. At the time, occasionally there used to be a faint thought in my mind that perhaps someday that young lady, 13 at the time, could be a match for me. I was about 21 at the time, so the thought was just a passing fancy; I would really try to shake off that sort of thinking—after all, she was a cousin-sister. However, cousin marriages are acceptable in many cultures, including Pakistan, India, Bangladesh, etc., as well as at least 20 states in the United States.

Perhaps my uncle and his wife had similar thoughts. But who could have guessed the future then! Oh yes, I remember, my uncle told me during this visit that he had the remaining balance of Rs.800/- with him from my late father's resources—a pleasant surprise and a most admirable evidence of his honesty. And he gave that amount to me to help me for my ambitious journey to the USA; that was a windfall!

And during my seven-year stay in the USA, I maintained occasional contact with this uncle. His letters were always affectionate, sympathetic about my struggles and encouraging about my goals and aspirations. As my years passed in the USA, sometimes I would ask him if Rukhsana needed something. The family had built a house in Lahore and moved there in the early 1960s. Rukhsana was now a college student. I would send her a book or something via someone returning to Lahore; one book I sent was Khalil Gibran's The Prophet, another was an encyclopedic dictionary. And also, a jewelry box once. I would get a nice "dear brother" thank-you note from her, also telling me how "everyone" missed me and admired me for my ambitions and for all that I was trying to accomplish. Of course, "everyone" included her as well. That was perhaps a suggestion. Rukhsana even sent me a charming 1964 picture of herself with one of these letters. Perhaps this was just an innocent gesture, perhaps it had some meaning; but enough to cause me to think in terms of a likely marital link. Was the picture sent with parental consent? Yes, I later found out, but only as an innocent gesture, I have been told.

3. Lahore Reconnections

After a few days in Karachi, I went to Lahore by train—flying was too expensive. I do not recall who received me at the railway station—probably the gang from for that old place, the dwelling of my mother-"step-father," was at the train-station to receive me. That was the place, even before I left for the USA, that used to be my breathing-space, though suffocating, whenever I came from Karachi for a few days. That was, of course, also the place from which I was discarded back in 1947, soon after we migrated from India. The receiving-group included, the "step-father," his adult son from the first wife, and my younger sister's husband, perhaps some others. For me, once again, it was a pretentiously "affectionate" re-connect with the monster.

Soon we arrived home. And there was my mother, emotional and in tears; and so was I. There were affectionate hugs and more tears. Whatever the early history, she was my mother, and she loved and cared; I was the prodigal son. There was the gap of my late father's love at age 4 and then the gap of my mother's love at age 10—all due to circumstances beyond my control. I am sure, as we arrived home, there were other people who came to see me from that complex, some of whom used to be fairly affectionate toward me—at least some elders who knew the early history of our misfortunes.

Soon we planned to visit my uncle and his family. As for my future wife, I am told that, while there was no love affair with me as such, but, just like myself, there was a seed in her heart about the marriage possibility—a seed planted simply by the knowledge that I was there and had often visited her household and, from early on, she admired me as one who was keen to enhance in life and desperate to overcome adversities. However, she would have acquiesced to parental wishes if I had not come along and someone else had entered the picture.

Here is how a more meaningful seed was planted.

Back in 1961, there was a news-item in Pakistani newspapers about my academic successes at Washington State University. Perhaps via the WSU news bureau, the news item appeared in a Pakistani newspaper, and it said,

> "Pullman, Wash., July 19, 1961—The Washington State University just published the list of students who achieved distinctive success. One among them is Shaikh M. Ghazanfar of Karachi. Ghazanfar is one of 912 undergraduate students who achieved distinctive success in studies during spring semester at this university of the Washington State."

One of our relatives saw this news item and passed on the clipping to some relatives, including my uncle's family in Lahore, and as he gave the clipping to my uncle, he said something to the effect that "Here is the news about Ghazanfar's successes in America." This fellow was keen to marry Rukhsana's elder sister, but there was no family reciprocity. And as he told Rukhsana about the clipping, he added, "Your father won't agree to my marriage with your sister, but I am sure he would give you to Ghazanfar in marriage." So, while the thought was already there, now it was further reinforced, I am told.

And there were other seedlings, I am told. Once

Rukhsana and her elder sister, while shopping, happened to encounter a sidewalk "fortune-teller" (still common in Lahore and elsewhere). And this individual told Rukhsana that someone from abroad will come and she will get married to him. And, at another time, so I am told, an elderly man, never seen before or after, happened to come to the door of the house, seeking some help. Rukhsana and her father went to the gate; and he looked at Rukhsana's feet, and said, "Daughter, your feet tell me you will be traveling far and abroad." The thought of her "traveling abroad" seemed another hint.

And, then suddenly I appear on the scene, from abroad, in July 1965.

4. Meeting My Future Bride

And, along with my mother, about mid-July or so, I visited my favorite uncle and his family in Lahore. This was after seven years, and I had matured and changed a bit—no longer the baby-face, now a bit heavier. And, I was told, I carried myself distinctly as though coming from abroad, and speaking the native language as though with an accent!! I was welcomed warmly by uncle, his wife, and the elder daughter. And then enters my future bride, Rukhsana, the young lady whom I last in 1958 when he was 13 years old. "Assalamo-Alaikum, Bhai Jan" ("Peace and Greetings, dear brother"). Soon also comes her 8-years old brother, Ameen, and he greeted me similarly. We all engaged in casual conversation, though with some strangeness when getting together after such a long time. Perhaps I talked about where I was in pursuing my own academic goals and my future plans, etc. I probably asked Rukhsana where she was in her studies and what was she studying.

Everyone was rather affectionate toward me. Perhaps

my mother hinted about my inclination to get married while visiting the homeland. There were perhaps repeat visits; perhaps I got some encouraging clues from the elder sister. Having visited a few times, I felt encouraged from my warm contacts with everyone, including Rukhsana.

5. Marriage Proposal: Mother Denied

As with my elder sister, my mother was also against the match; but I persuaded her to explore for me with her brother. And she did. And she received a flat no; the brother rebuked her: "How dare you ask! You want my daughter for your son and then take her to that rascal's house? No way. Just forget it." The cultural tradition is that after marriage, the couple goes first to the groom's house—that being the house where I was staying, i.e., the household of my mother and the rascal "step-father," the murderer of my father. Besides, I was still in the ugly shadow of my decades-old double-life.

And then began my own mission. I was reasonably confident that Rukhsana was inclined toward marrying me, including some clues from the elder sister, and there were expressions of lavish love from the household, especially Rukhsana's mother. Also, I learnt from my lovely wife that, years ago, when I used to visit the family at Kasur, she had heard of my struggles and my determination to accomplish things in life; and she had always felt an innocent sense of admiration for me.

6. Marriage: Direct Approach

Having learnt of some positive vibrations, I felt encouraged; I decided to take the direct approach.

Soon after, I sat down with my uncle, and I politely expressed my desire for his daughter's hand in marriage.

His response was encouraging, but how could it be when I was still a student? How would we survive as a married couple? And then where would the couple go for the next few days after marriage? Obviously, he didn't want us to spend any time in my mother's household. He suggested that I should wait till I return upon completion of my doctorate and that perhaps a simple engagement now and marriage upon return. I resisted that notion, for, I remember, I told him that here I was 28 years old and have had enough of bachelor living and I was ready to settle down and share my life with a suitable wife. And Rukhsana is the one; and I indicated that I thought our feelings were mutual. I remember having relied on hints from the elder sister that Rukhsana was inclined toward marriage at this time. Besides, there were all those predictions of this marriage, before my appearance, from that sooth-sayer and from that someone who had stopped at the house door; and that family relative, who shared the 1961 newspaper clipping about me, had told Rukhsana that I would be the one.

And I told my uncle, Rukhsana's father, that I was not inclined to return unmarried to the USA. He queried about various aspects of life in the USA, understandable questions from the perspective of a father. I am sure I also told him that I was at a stage where I was ready for a complete disconnect with the monster of our lives. Moreover, I told him, I intended soon to confront the monster and that I would tolerate whatever the suffering he would, as a result, inflict upon my mother. And, further, if we were married, we won't be spending any time in that household; instead, we would, to maintain the tradition, briefly go, as married couple, to my younger sister's house.

And then another interrogation process. This exploratory task was assigned to my uncle's son-in-law, the husband of another older sister. If we get married and move to the U.S.A., how will we survive economically when I am still a student? I assured him and everyone else that this was hardly a matter of concern in the U.S., for there were so many married couples, often full-time students, managing themselves rather well, through part-time work, scholarships, borrowing, etc. In our case, I assured him, we would be reasonably "well-off," for I will have a graduate assistantship which would pay enough to live comfortably. Remember this was summer 1965, and most people in Pakistan, even the educated ones, had no comprehension of life, especially student life, in the U.S.A. Moreover, often people heard of disasters where someone comes from abroad, gets married here, followed by disastrous discoveries that the man was already married abroad or had girl-friends. I must have provided my good-faith assurances in such respects. And, yes, I had to make another commitment to my in-laws—that we would return after four years, and then try to settle in Pakistan.

7.   Marriage Agreed

In any case, after all such interrogations, my uncle happily consented to the marriage proposal and the marriage would take place now. My mother was unhappy, for her own proposal to the brother was rejected. Further, I am sure I must have hinted to her that the monster won't belong in this event, whatever the consequences. If he would prevent her from attending the event, she would suffer, and I would suffer, but that I would have to accept. After all, that was the man she had married after my own father's "sudden demise." And, of course, she was aware of the cruelties and abuse that we the orphaned children suffered at his hands, as, indeed, she did too.

The marriage proposal having been settled, now the work began as to all the logistics. During this time, both Rukhsana and I were 'permitted' to move around together and visit some friends if we wished to. Once we went to a local park, accompanied by the elder sister as our chaperon. However, as we reached the park, we asked her to allow us to have our own private conversation; she cooperated. We both sat in the park for a couple of hours and talked of our future together. I wanted her to know me a bit more—and vice versa. We both realized that one really learns about each other after marriage when intimate living together begins; and we both believed that if commitments are strong, married life ought to work out just fine.

The date was set for Saturday, August 16, 1965. Of course, I didn't have much in terms of finances, and resources were limited on the other side as well. An extravagant marriage, with all the various celebratory events, was not at all possible; and, as a matter of principle, I personally was not at all inclined toward that kind of extravaganza.

However, now comes the confrontation with the monster—and then the marriage.

Chapter XI

CONFRONTING THE MONSTER; OUR MARRIAGE

During the next few days, I was still staying at my mother's household, in the presence of the "step-father." However, during my presence here, I had alerted my mother that I intended to have a conversation with the monster; she was vehemently against it, and I could understand her fears. I was absolutely determined, however. I would face the monster, but I would give him a cold shoulder. Let me once again express my fear, the sort I always felt even when visiting the household, as a youngster before migration from India and also whenever I stayed in this environment: what if the monster decides to get rid of me? I used to have that anxiety, especially when going to sleep. I felt that anxiety even now.

1. Confronting the Monster

So, one afternoon, a few days before our wedding date (August 16, 1965), I told my "step-father" that I wished to talk to him. He had some suspicion about it, for I was usually a bit reserved with him and perhaps mother had given him some hint.

We were both in a room, and I closed the doors. He had no choice but to listen. I believe mother also entered the room.

I began by asking, "Why you did what you did to my father?"

"What did I do, what did I do?" he answered, pretending ignorance.

"You know very well; everyone in the clan and in the world knows what you did—and you ask what did you do? And what you did to the rest of us?"

And then mother entered the room, with extreme anxiety, "Son, leave it all aside, whatever happened, happened, leave it aside; it's all history now."

And then I asked, "You murdered my father and you ruined our lives, including the lives of my sisters. Do you remember all that? Do you want to acknowledge all that? Tell me, tell me!"

He was mumbling, "nothing, nothing; it is all history, bygones, bygone. You are my son......"

"O please, do not call me your son; just think about it, after all that you did to us—how can you think of yourself as my 'father.' I absolutely do not—no more. No way..... you know damn well I have lived a lie all my life, having to respect you, to obey you, to finance your household and your whims during the years I worked in Karachi, and even comply by your whims and finance your needs while I was starving in America, for you would otherwise be brutal, as you have been always, to this woman, my mother. She lived a life of lies, as we all had to. But no more, no more, whatever the consequences."

He just listened, a bit stunned.

And, moreover, "I am getting married soon to my uncle's daughter, and that's the man who, for what you did to his sister's husband and family, also has despised you all his life. And you are not going to set foot, not even your shadow, in that event. If you want to prevent my mother from being part of her son's marriage, so be it. I will tolerate."

And, "whomever else you want to prevent from this event, you are free to do; I don't care." I was thinking of my sisters, of course—including the half-sister and half-brother, as well as others in that clan.

"But I am done—I have suffered enough all my life. Because of what you did, my own late father has not been part of my life from age four and he can't be at his only son's marriage because of what you did; there is no way on earth that I want to see your face at that event, whatever, whatever the consequences. I am absolutely done with you, no more and no longer do I want to see your face ever."

He was a bit reactive, but mostly just mumbling. I know I must have been crying out loud from my own pain and agony during this conversation, as I am at this moment while narrating all this. I know my mother was also screaming and crying: "don't, son, don't." Here it was—the decades-old pandora's box finally exploded by me. No more pretentions, no more fake living.

A huge load off my mind; such a relief. It is done, finally. I am free now, at last. And I remember, in that same household, I said special prayers, in thanks to God Almighty and for His mercy, as I was soon to be a married man, getting married to someone with whom I felt there was some mutuality of attraction; and I cried bitterly while sitting on the prayer-mat, remembering and missing my late father, reflecting about my life, and thanking God Almighty for granting me some success in this worldly life, and most importantly, thanking Him for my forthcoming marriage to someone for whom, I knew, there was enormous mutual love. And I prayed solemnly for making ours a successful, eternal marriage. My mother saw me in that state and perhaps wondered; perhaps I explained to her why.

But there were still anxieties. I was still spending the next few days and nights in that household, till the marriage took place. What if the monster, the criminal mind that he was, decided to murder me, or have me murdered? He did it to my father, why not the son now? What if he tried to create other obstacles to make my life difficult in the next few days, including perhaps trying to sabotage the marriage? What if he forced my mother and my sister so they could not attend the marriage event? Obviously, during these next few days, my contact with him was non-existent; I would absolutely want to avoid any face-to-face contact with him, even though I did spend part of my next few days and nights in that house. I was, however, connecting with some others in that clan—including his son from the first wife. Somehow, as a grown-up man, his son understood the circumstances and he perhaps even appreciated my position, for everyone knew, especially the elders, what his father had been all about. In fact, everyone lived the lies about that man all these decades; but none could ever confront him. And he always presented himself as the noble, pious man in the clan and among his friends and neighbors.

2. The Sacred Bond: Our Marriage

Here I was now, ready to embark on the most unique relationship of the human family, sanctified by God Almighty as the most sacred bond between a man and a woman—my marriage to the lovely lady of my choice; and her marriage to the man of her choice.

The wedding date was set for Saturday, August 16, 1965. The groom will come from the house of my younger sister, which was not far away. Once married, the couple will also return to the same house. A bit unusual, but so what; those customs hardly mattered to me, nor did they matter much to my bride and in-laws. For we were about to enter into the noble bond between a man and a woman, most loving, sincere and with all the good intensions. Customs and rituals didn't matter much.

On August 16, 1965, the few family members, as well as the groom, were gathered at my sister's house; this was the groom's "wedding party' ('baraat') place. From here, the party went back in horse-driven carriages ("tonga's") to my uncle's house where the bride and other guests awaited our arrival. What is most notable here is the fact that, much to my joy and satisfaction, my mother was also there for the event. I learnt later that the monster's grown-up son from the first wife played a key role in that respect; he confronted his father and told him not to prevent my mother, or anyone else, from joining the marriage ceremonies. Also, my half-sister and her family joined the ceremonies, apparently despite her father's admonitions. Unfortunately, my elder sister and her family, who lived in Karachi, also could not join.

Once the group arrived at the bride's house, there were several other relatives, friends, and neighbors to welcome. Among the friends were my dearest friends from school days, Asif and Mushahid. I persuaded them and they wanted to join; they came from Karachi, 700 miles away. Th other uncle was there, as well as my cousin (whom I discovered while attending Washington State University) and several friends, as well as a few from the clan. Of course, there were the families of my uncle's married daughters.

The religious marriage nuptial ('nikah') ceremony was a most somber occasion. It was in the afternoon, hot days of the tropical summer, in the living room of the house, with several male members present, family and guests. The bride, along with female members, family and guests, was in another room of the house, as the cultural norms warranted. As the 'nikah' took place, I was in tears, overwhelmed with an avalanche of emotions—my bride, my new life, my new family links, and above all, I was missing my late father. Here I go—my tears again as I write. 'Nikah' took place—and then prayers, congratulations, embraces, good wishes, etc. My uncle, now father-in-law, with tears in his eyes, gave me a wedding ring, with our initials engraved on the inside, my prized treasure. And then, the two of us— bride and groom—sat on chairs, next to each other, in the courtyard of the house; numerous pictures were taken with close family members. Several group pictures with members of the family and friends were taken in front of the house.

Back to the marriage. Now the 'departure' ('rukhsati') ceremony. Perhaps some tears were shed by those present, culturally relevant, of course. And then in a well-decorated car that belonged to a good friend, my bride and I, along with my sister, and Rukhsana's elder sister, turned around and came to my sister's house, chosen as the 'groom's' house—the same house from where we started a few hours earlier. My shy bride, in her elegant bridal dress, sat on the bed, as the ladies, even from neighborhood, peaked at her charming face. I sat with male guests in the adjacent room.

The usual 'departure' is to the house of the groom, where the married couple will spend their bridal night. There was no such house for us, and my sister's house was extremely small. So, my now father-in-law, had made arrangements with a neighborhood friend and a bedroom in that house had been decorated for us to spend our bridal night. Later in the evening, we left my sister's house and took the horse-driven carriage to go to that house. A side note is in order here. Being a complete novice, and having lived abroad for seven years, I was unaware of so many traditions—one was about giving a special gift to the bride on that special night. I must have talked of this with friends, and, of course, my finances were very meager. I bought a special perfume for my bride (brand-name **4711**), quite well-known during those days—and I presented that to my bride on that first night. In retrospect, I have been told, it wasn't much of a "special" gift; regardless, however, it is part of our memory.

And how about that special night? We simply talked and talked that first night; and I was especially concerned about the emotional state of my bride, the pleasant transition of moving to a new life with me, though known to her for years, yet a stranger in so many ways. What is in store for her—and for me, in our common future? Our special night became our next night, which was back in that same room where our betrothal took place the previous day—my now in-laws house; and that night we were truly each other's conjugal mates. Next afternoon, there was a small gathering of close relatives and friends in the house where we spent the previous night; and unlike the usual lavish dinner service, tea and some refreshments were served to the guests; I was quite satisfied with the simplicity.

And, during the next few days, we visited relatives. Also, I asked my uncle if the two of us could briefly visit my mother's house, for several acquaintances there were keen to see the two of us. His gracious answer was something like this: "You both are husband and wife now; I am OK with whatever you both together decide to do; it is your life; I will not impose my will." Yet, with his permission, we went there a couple of times—and there were the monster's relatives who visited to see us. I don't recall if the monster also was around; however, I know I must have absolutely shunned him. My bride remembers, however, that there was exchange of formal greetings with him. And, again, there was that lingering anxiety, lest he decides to harm me and my bride.

We spent the next few days at my in-laws' house. Several friends visited us. One good friend took us to a historic garden and he made a silent movie of that excursion; Asif and Mushahid were part of that excursion, of course. That movie is part of our treasured possessions.

3. Our Honeymoon

And then, a few days later, we proceeded for our honeymoon to a resort town, Murree, about 300 miles north of Lahore. And here is something for the memories: I persuaded my dear friends, Asif and Mushahid, to also accompany us to our honeymoon!! Four of us took the train to Rawalpindi, on way to Murree via a bus the next day. There was an interesting incident in the train. The four of us sat together in the train, Rukhsana on my right and Asif-Mushahid on my left. Rather casually, sometimes I would touch my wife on the arm or put my around her shoulders, not realizing that I was in the Pakistan's traditional culture where such gestures in public are viewed as vulgar. Soon, a bearded, elderly person, sitting in front of us, holding an infant baby of his own, started yelling at us: we were scoundrels, we were acting as though we were kidnappers of this girl, etc. After some heated exchange, things calmed down. And soon the bearded man, who had threatened to have us thrown out of the train at the next stop, decided to move elsewhere; and I learned my lesson.

Once in Rawalpindi, we visited some relatives there.

Then all four of us proceeded to Murree. The few nights in Murree were rather unique and memorable. Here is a young, newly-wed couple, also accompanied by friends! All four of us checked into a hotel, with our separate rooms, of course. But there was the consciousness of our nights together as newly-weds. And next day, the bachelors, Asif and Mushahid, would express their curiosity and ask some loaded questions about our nights. The two of us alone did go for walks in the Murree hills and took many pictures. And the beautiful memories are always fresh.

We returned to Lahore after a few days. Soon, my dear friends returned to Karachi.

And we began our plans for our travel to the USA, especially the visa for my new bride.

Chapter XII

RETURN TO THE USA; UNFORESEEN HURDLES

Soon after our wedding, I had initiated the process for our departure together to the USA—Rukhsana's passport, visa, travel arrangements, etc. We had obtained the passport, but visa was needed to enter the U.S. I went to the U.S. Consulate for that purpose and I produced all the documents for myself: valid passport, return-visa, admission in the doctorate program, and a teaching assistantship with evidence of my monthly income. With all that evidence, the Consulate readily issued a dependent-F2 visa for Rukhsana. We were set to travel.

Now the travel plans. I had my round-trip ticket from the USA, but Rukhsana's travel had to be arranged so that it would coincide with mine. My own resources being quite meager, Rukhsana's father somehow managed to buy her airline ticket for the USA. Everything set to go. And so, early in September 1965, we proceeded by train to Karachi. I remember there was a large crowd of loved ones to see us off at the train station; after all, we were heading to the USA. And then, after a few days, we were set to depart for the USA on September 7th—I had my charter-return flight via London, and my bride was booked on a PIA flight to London and then join me there on a BOAC flight (part of my charter-flight) to New York airport.

After reaching Karachi, we proceeded directly to my sister's house, where we planned to stay till our flight on September 7th. Later, my in-laws and the other daughter came to Karachi, by train, to see us off for our journey to the USA. They were picked up by Rukhsana's maternal uncle, a senior army official; and they stayed in his house. These were intensely emotional connections; the aged parents were soon to part with their married daughter, not likely to see her for the next few years.

1.   Karachi: Visiting Friends and Relatives

During the next few days, we visited my aunt's family, with my beautiful bride, Rukhsana, whose father (aunt's brother) had had a lifelong disconnect with the sister. For the first time, Rukhsana met this aunt (my maternal, of course) and her cousins. It was quite a memorable visit, though we both sensed the welcome was a bit subdued. I could understand why, given the historic family disconnect with Rukhsana's father.

Then we also visited Asif's household where I spent so much time during earlier years; that was family. That house was the source of so much affection and encouragement, at a time when I was yearning for such connections. And we visited Mushahid's family as well. At that time, Mushahid lived with his parents at that old one-room house where also I received so much affection. Fate has brought me, after so many years, to the same place where Mushahid and I, as high-school students, used to study underneath the staircase, aided by the dim light of a kerosene lamp. Those connections were so meaningful for me, and I never can forget that, and I am so grateful. And they welcomed my bride with such affection. A most welcoming environment for both of us, indeed.

2. Hurdles: Travel Uncertainty

As fate would have it, a rather unpredictable event took place that threatened to seriously affect our travel plans. My plan was to return to Washington State University, Pullman, where I was to resume my doctorate program, beginning the fall semester, 1965. I had my student-visa to return, and Rukhsana had her dependent-visa to accompany me.

And there was the hurdle; w*ar broke out between India and Pakistan on September 5, 1965; and we were to fly out on September 7th.* All airline traffic was suspended indefinitely; there were blackouts and sounds of sirens every night. One could hear the sounds of fighter-planes at night; there were rumors of bombings from Indian fighter-planes. This went on for the next several days.

Our September 7th departure plans were no more. During this time, we both felt like abandoned children. If I cannot return to WSU this semester, where will we go? What will I do here for the next several months—with no job in Pakistan and the responsibility of a wife now?? Now all my energies were focusing on how we could manage to leave the country; and time was not quite in our favor, for the semester at WSU was to start around mid-September. Not only I had to resume my academics but also take the responsibilities of teaching. And to find a place to live upon our arrival at Pullman, Washington. Obviously, there was anxiety beyond belief.

During the next few days, we both were like nomads— one night here, one night there; and nights, especially, were scary because of blackouts and the fear of bombs dropping.

We stayed a couple of nights at the house of Asif's elder brother whose wedding I attended the previous month. Then, we also stayed a night or two at Asif's apartment near his place of employment. I remember Mushahid would also come there in the evenings. And, the four of us would reminisce nostalgically about our lives and discuss various options as to how we could travel under new circumstances.

As the war fever abated somewhat in the next few days, some air flights were allowed—especially for government officials and business folks. Of course, my charter-flight return flight was history. Rukhsana's ticket was OK, however. Being absolutely penniless, how do I arrange my return flight now? This is where Mushahid's friendship became our strength. He was employed in a senior position with a commercial bank. He found out that if I could somehow purchase my ticket in dollars, instead of rupees, then perhaps things could work out. But how do I do that? Well, Mushahid managed to make arrangements with officials of the State Bank of Pakistan (Pakistan's Central Bank) that the ticket could be purchased in rupees, with his written guarantee that the dollar equivalent would be remitted soon after my arrival in the USA. That was his pledge to the State Bank in my behalf and, of course, my pledge that I would remit the dollar amount soon after our return to the U.S.

3. New Travel Plans and Exit

Having worked out our revised travel plans, we both had the airline tickets, with New York as our destination, via London. But how do we get a flight when the only flights leaving Karachi are for government officials and business folks?

With contacts here and there, we received some assurance that if we would get to the airport for a certain departing flight, perhaps we would get in, if some other passengers did not show up. We did just that one evening but came back disappointed. Then again, the next evening, probably around September 9th or so; and it worked! I remember we were handed boarding passes with names of passengers who did not show up. Of course, lights were dim and darkness outside. As we boarded the plane, we were quite apprehensive and everyone in the plane was praying for a safe flight, for, with blackout and occasional sound of sirens, there was the fear of a bomb strike. Our plane took off and we were relieved when the plane reached a certain altitude and was outside the Pakistan skies.

And we reached London after a few hours. We were warmly received by a long-time good friend, who had been informed of our arrival schedule. We stayed with him for a couple of days. I was keen to ascertain details about our flights to New York. I found out that the London-New York segment of my charter-flight remained intact, but I was now placed on some other flight, but Rukhsana couldn't travel on that charter-flight. There was no choice except to arrange her flight on another airline and she would fly by herself from London to New York. We worked it out so she would arrive at the New York airport a few hours after my flight's arrival and I would be there to receive her. What a challenge for a young, naïve bride of mine who had hardly ever set foot outside of her house alone—and now having to travel alone across the Atlantic! Anyway, she was willing and bold enough to go through the challenge. And she did. The date was perhaps September 12th.

4. New York Arrival

We reached New York, but not without another mishap. My departure flight was a bit delayed. And, contrary to what I had arranged, I arrived a few hours late and Rukhsana was already there! I wasn't there to greet her at the New York airport, as she thought I would be; huge insecurity for her. Fortunately, however, it so happened that a good friend (my dormitory roommate from undergraduate days) and his wife were also traveling around New York City—and I had communicated to them it would be nice to get together with them at the airport when we arrived, so they could meet my bride.

Well, they did come, but I wasn't there. However, they spotted the exotically-dressed, somewhat lost and confused young woman—and they connected with her and introduced themselves as my friends. What a relief for her and what a wonderful gesture on the part of my good friends. After this airport rendezvous with her, I too arrived a few hours later; and we thanked my friends profusely. Then the couple left and resumed their own travels.

Soon after I arrived, I found that several friends from Providence and Boston had also come to the airport to welcome us. And all of us traveled back to Providence, Rhode Island; that's where I had left behind my old car and my personal belongings. We informed all loved ones in Pakistan that we had arrived at our destination safe and sound. And we stayed one or two nights with a very cordial East Pakistani (now Bangladeshi) family. All my friends took us out one evening for a welcoming dinner party. Those wonderful friendships have survived the test of time.

I knew that my arrival at Washington State University would be delayed by a few days, so I informed the department there and they understood.

And, of course, I also had to meet my pledge to my friend, Mushahid, whose contacts enabled the purchase of Rukhsana's airline ticket in U.S. dollars, and the dollar amount had to be remitted soon after our arrival. I managed to borrow the requisite amount from my local bank and remitted it to my friend.

5. Driving to Pullman, Washington

All my personal belongings were stored in the apartment where I lived while a student at Brown University. And there was my junky old car, 1958 Chevrolet, reasonably functional; we intended to drive back to Pullman in that car. Of course, I had driven across country before, but this was to be a uniquely enjoyable experience of sight-seeing in the company of my lovely wife. And I didn't have much in terms of resources—not much money, nor my own camera. I remember I borrowed some money from a good friend and borrowed a camera from another. In any case, I loaded up the car with our luggage—trunk, back-seat, leg-room area, absolutely packed. In fact, we fixed the back seat of car in the shape of a little bed so that Rukhsana could lie down and relax there if needed. I was the only driver, of course.

As we embarked on this journey, perhaps around September 14th or so, we decided to first go to Niagara Falls, one of the most attractive natural wonders where newly-weds are known to go for their honeymoon. We went there and took the sights and then on to Toronto. In Toronto, we visited my friend, Asif's sister and brother—affectionate part of my Karachi days of youth. They welcomed the newly-weds with utmost warmth. And while driving from Niagara Falls to Toronto, we passed through a town called London, Ontario. And Rukhsana asked, "Are we still in England."

That blooper-story of my naïve, young bride has been repeated many times.

And after a day or so, we resumed our west-ward travel, with Pullman as our destination. And it was a very fast trip. Short of resources, we slept for a night or two in the car while parked in some rest-area or a national park along the way. Other nights in some inexpensive motels. We carried some food and snacks in the car. And often we stopped at drive-in stands for hamburgers and drinks. Sometimes we would pick up the food and eat at a rest-area or alongside the highway somewhere. These were all new experiences for my wife. I drove each day for perhaps 10-12 hours. There were beautiful sights all along. I remember having some minor car trouble in Cedar Rapids, Iowa. Other than that, our junky car did fine all the way to Pullman.

We drove through the Dakotas—saw the sights of the beautiful, colorful geological topography of the Badlands and then drove through the Mt. Rushmore National Park, where there are the famous Presidential monuments, carved in the mountain. I recalled my September 1958 Greyhound bus travel from New York to Pullman and at the time I really could not appreciate the scenic sights and places. That also seemed to be the case for my bride; the long travel was not all that enjoyable—except that we were together. One really must live in the USA for a while to be able to enjoy and internalize the various fascinating sights in this land.

6. Arrival in Pullman

We arrived in Pullman, perhaps around September 19th or so, just in time for resuming my academics at WSU. We spent the first couple of nights with some friends who lived in the married students housing near the campus. Those apartments were allowed for rental to Pakistani exchange-students who found university dormitories less desirable for their living style. Those were rather flimsily constructed rows of apartments, built at one time as army barracks; yet they were good enough for student housing, and, most importantly, very low rental value! We were able to rent a 2-bedroom apartment. It was semi-furnished (meaning an old refrigerator, cooking range, and a kitchen table with four chairs), with a monthly rent of about $50.00!

We had to arrange the rest of the furnishings, and our resources were meager. I borrowed some money from the bank to get us started. Gradually, we bought some furnishings, all used items—a mattress set (no frame!), another mattress only for the second room, a dresser, and a couple of chairs. A faculty-friend gave us a used covered sofa (which had some cuts in the middle, which I somehow glued together!). We also found a used, single sofa chair— not very pretty, but good enough and rather large so even both of us could fit in it! Also, we found a center table from somewhere, as well as a study-table, chair, table-lamps, etc. for the second room, which was to be my study room. We bought some pots and pans for our kitchen, and yes, a plastic set of dishes. Also, some bed-sheets, pillows, etc., as well as other household supplies. Some such items came as gifts to the newly-married couple. Of course, we had our old car in which we traveled all the way from Rhode Island.

We were pretty much set to begin our new, rather modest, married student household—I, the student, and Rukhsana, the housewife, at least for now. She hardly knew any cooking, but that didn't matter to us. She learnt things in time, with my help (I had learnt some cooking, having lived as a bachelor for some years) and with the help of friends, and of course, instructions in letters from her mother. We managed just fine.

Soon, various Pakistani friends invited the newly-weds for dinner gatherings at their apartments. At one of these gatherings, there was this discovery: another cousin discovered in my odyssey, the son of my father's sister. We hugged each other, and I probably cried, for here was another close link to my late father.

7. Our Married Life

During these early months of our life together, we regularly assured our families, especially my in-laws, that we were just fine—we were happily living together, adjusting wonderfully to each other as a married couple. Obviously, there were understandable anxieties on the part of my in-laws; after all, there I was—appearing suddenly, after seven years abroad, and then the rather hurriedly-arranged marriage to their young, innocent daughter, who at the time had just completed her bachelor's degree. None was prepared for things happening that rapidly, but they did and within a few weeks of my connection with the family, we were now married and living in the United States. Especially, during those days, that was quite a dramatic transformation for everyone; that was the time when about the only means of communications were letters and it took about a month for exchange of letters! And telephone links were almost impossible.

There were also our own adjustment trials, especially Rukhsana's. Of course, she was new to the cultural environment here, and there was a lot to learn and assimilate. She met several American families in Pullman whom I had known for years: Ted and Jean Saldin, Jack and Ida Guthrie, and some others. They welcomed us warmly and they occasionally invited us for dinners and other get-togethers. Also, Dr. Edna Douglas, my mentor for whom I worked part-time as an undergraduate and as her research assistant during the master's degree program, welcomed us enthusiastically. These families also gave us gifts for our new household. Also, there were frequent interactions with the Pakistani families and individuals.

All such connections gradually enabled Rukhsana to be more comfortable, more at ease with the environment here, and less homesick. And, also we both were now gradually more accustomed to each other—both of us adjusting and adapting to each other's whims and idiosyncrasies. I should add that, in retrospect, I was perhaps more demanding; I was the teacher and the guide, as well as the husband and the breadwinner.

There were times when we would have some arguments, she would cry and feel insecure. However, I would always assure her that we could argue all we want, be angry with each other, and perhaps not even talk to each other for a couple of days. *But, please, do not ever think that I would want to abandon and let go of you; that thought would never enter my mind; please be absolutely sure of that solid, solemn commitment on my part.* Thanks God Almighty, while we have had our ups and downs, just like most couples, we have lived a wonderful life as a married couple and as a family.

During this first year of our lives together, while I was a full-time graduate student and half-time teaching assistant, Rukhsana was pretty much a housewife. We had bought an old black-and-white TV for her entertainment and also to get more at ease with the English language here. During these months, she also did some babysitting for some extra income. Given her dependent-visa, she could not work anywhere else. However, she had plans to be a student here and work toward another degree in her field of psychology;

and I too was keen that she ought to pursue higher studies in this land.

We visited the Ratliffs (parents of my good friend from the first week of my 1958 arrival!) at the first opportunity, perhaps during Thanksgiving break. Of course, they welcomed my bride with utmost affection. We also traveled to Seattle and Portland to visit Pakistani and American friends, and, of course, to enjoy various scenic spots and places—the drive through the scenic mountains, water-falls, the Space Needle in Seattle, and various sights in Portland, Oregon, and return-drive on the scenic highway along the Columbia River, and of course, the famous Multnomah Falls along the way.

8. Our Student Life

The fall semester began, and I was occupied with the courses to be completed toward my doctorate, and also, I was teaching two sections of an introductory economics course, part of my responsibilities as a teaching assistant. I had an office on the campus and often Rukhsana would walk there so we could enjoy our lunch together. She was gradually becoming familiar with life here, especially campus life.

Rukhsana and I were keen that she ought to enhance her academic credentials. To enroll as a student, her visa needed to be converted to an F-1 visa, to be an independent student. We had obtained the originals of her academic credentials from Pakistan. Just so that she would gradually orient herself to the demands of education here, she took just a couple of courses during the first semester. She completed them quite successfully and was now ready to enroll on a full-time basis. Based on her academic work from Pakistan, she was accorded advanced credit for two years toward the bachelor's degree and granted admission, effective fall 1966.

To admitted as a full-time student, it was also essential that we must provide evidence of enough financial capability for her; my income as a teaching-assistant would not do. That became an obstacle, but, thank God for some of my American mentors and well-wishers. During summer 1966, I worked full-time as a research assistant in the WSU's Bureau of Economics and Business Research, with Dr. Guthrie as the Director. I had worked for the Bureau even earlier, as an undergraduate and as a graduate student during spring 1964-65. Dr. Guthrie knew me very well and often expressed admiration for my work-ethic and my determination to excel in things I pursued, academic or others. By this time, the Guthrie family had also come to know Rukhsana rather well.

So, I approached Dr. Guthrie if he could possibly give the financial assurance for my wife, so she could be a full-time student. He knew me quite well and understood that we would not allow our situation to ever become a burden upon him. After all, I came here, back in September 1958, almost penniless, and I somehow survived—and he knew it and appreciated my efforts to succeed; and now the two of us, as students, shall survive, indeed. I had my regular income as a teaching assistant which ought to be enough for us to manage our household, plus perhaps Rukhsana too could work part-time. Besides, the WSU Foreign Students Office had assured us of the out-of-state fee waiver for her—a huge help toward our finances; I too had that waiver during my undergraduate years.

Dr. Guthrie agreed to provide the financial assurance for Rukhsana's student status—a formality to be fulfilled for the U.S. Immigration to convert her visa to an F-1 student visa. Indeed, a gracious gesture on his part. I always think of the late Guthries with utmost respect and gratitude. During summer 1966, Rukhsana's visa was converted to a student-visa from the dependent-visa.

Now Rukhsana was eligible to be a full-time student in her own right, effective fall 1966, to work toward a bachelor's degree in psychology. WSU had given her approximately two-years of credit for the bachelor's degree earned in Pakistan, which was the standard practice during those days (unlike nowadays when about any bachelor's degree from anywhere is often good enough to be directly admitted as a graduate student! Why? Not only the academic standards in the USA have declined tremendously, but, for budgetary reasons, universities are anxious to recruit students!). So, effective fall 1966-67, we were both full-time students. Wonderful!

I had a teaching assistantship, of course, with my office and in the same building was Rukhsana's Pyschology Department. She had some of her classes in the same vicinity, as I did. Since she also had to complete some core courses (mathematics, physics, geology, plus some others), they required her to go to other buildings on the campus. So now we had a new routine. We would often walk together to the campus, take our lunch bags with us, eat together in my office, and then walk back together to our apartment. Sometime, because of our schedule, we would be walking back and forth separately.

Of course, throughout, there was considerable learning and adaptation for her—campus environment different from Pakistan, different teaching styles, different learning styles, periodic tests with courses segmented into components for the semester; rote memorization, as common in Pakistan, just won't do. And there was also the cold, snowy weather to get used to; once or twice, she slipped on the snow, but managed OK. Our life was quite busy, very busy indeed.

But I was determined, as she was. Pressure to succeed, do well and maintain at least a B average.

Later, as she became a bit comfortable about things, we looked for a part-time job for her. She found some work with the WSU Computer Department, filling computer cards with data and then those cards would be fed into the computer for analysis. Later, there was also another few-hours job in the Entomology Lab, counting bugs and butterflies and tacking them on cardboards. Very interesting!! In the evenings, sometimes we would study in the library, but more often at home. She would be busy in her studies and I would be occupied in the other room, studying intensively for my doctoral examinations, scheduled for late Spring 1967. Both of us used to be thoroughly occupied. Only occasionally, we would have some social life—weekends or during breaks.

Rukhsana completed her fall 1966-67 semester quite successfully; now she was in the routine of things. Taking tests, writing term-papers, etc. I used to insist that she ought to learn typing (we had an old portable typewriter!) and even got her a lessons-book. She tried and learned the methods somewhat. Sometimes I would type her term-papers; other times, she would neatly hand-write the work.

During spring 1967, I took my doctorate examinations. This was the most critical phase of my academic life, the key step toward the ultimate academic milestone, the doctorate degree. Would I do well? What if I fail? Extremely tense and hectic times. I took the exams., spread over two weeks, eight subjects to cover and the candidates would be given one whole day to write answers to the questions in each subject. There were the written exams., and then the oral defense. I passed in flying colors, or so I was told. Thanks God Almighty—I was nearer to my doctorate goal.

Now the dissertation work would be pursued in a relatively relaxed manner during academic 1967-68. And the Department now offered me a Lectureship, a step up from being a Teaching Assistant. My wife was overjoyed; we sent telegrams to my in-laws and perhaps to my sister. But during all these milestones, I would often also think of my late father. I wanted to scream so my late father could hear of his son's success. How proud he would feel of his only son—so closely to achieving the pinnacle of scholarship.

Rukhsana also successfully completed her spring semester course work. Now she was quite accustomed to the study routine, used to the academic environment, quite comfortable in communications and interpersonal connections with faculty and others around. Things moving along quite smoothly for us and we were rather well adjusted to each other. She was well on her way to successfully earning her second bachelor's degree—and then perhaps work toward a master's degree. I was comfortably on course to completing my doctorate degree and now searching for a suitable research topic for the dissertation, to be pursued and completed for award of the doctorate degree.

Also, I am in the market for a suitable faculty position somewhere, as assistant professor of economics. Meantime, I had a summer job with the Department's Economics and Business Research Bureau. However, we were also inclined to do some recreational traveling later during the summer.

Chapter XIII

OUR CHILDREN, MY JOB, PAKISTAN VISITS

While I had cleared my doctoral exams., the dissertations research was still in progress and we continued to live in Pullman, Washington. And Rukhsana was well on her way to completing her bachelor's degree at the end of the spring semester, 1968.

By this time, we had acquired another used car, which seemed rather reliable for longer journeys. We periodically took time off during summers and other short breaks for excursion travel. During late summer 1966, we took a camping trip to Canada, enjoying the sights along the way— Glacier National Park (Canada side), then on to the most scenic Banff National Park in Canada.

Then during summer 1967, accompanied by another couple, we took a longer trip—along the coastal highway, from Oregon to Southern California and returned via Nevada, Arizona, Utah, and then back to Idaho. I had visited many of the scenic spots earlier, but now the difference was this: I was accompanied by my lovely wife and I wanted her to enjoy the sights.

During our travels, Rukhsana would sometimes

complain of being unusually tired and nauseous. We assumed it was simply travel fatigue. Soon the mystery was happily solved.

1. Our Daughter Coming

Upon return home, Rukhsana continued to complain about being tired and lethargic. So, she took a pregnancy test, just in case. Indeed, she was pregnant! While we both wanted to complete our academic goals and then have a family, but the news was pure ecstasy! Our first child on the way!! The doctor encouraged Rukhsana to be reasonably active, continue her classes, and that we need not be concerned about the healthy development of our baby. It was such a unique joy to experience the gradual growth of our baby.

Rukhsana being rather small (about 110 pounds or so at the time), the growth was not too conspicuously visible, even late in pregnancy. And, once a neighborhood friend jokingly said, "Looks like you are going to have an olive for a baby!" And that was devastating for us to hear, especially for the soon-to-be mother. However, the gynecologist assured us that the baby was growing just fine. We were told that the approximate date for the birth would be about mid-late May. Rukhsana's final exams were scheduled during early June 1968 and convocation on Saturday, June 9, 1968.

And the day arrived. Born at Memorial Hospital, Pullman, Washington, on Sunday, May 26, 1968, at 1.24 p.m., our dearest, our only daughter, Farah Noreen Ghazanfar (always my 'Fari-Pari') entered and blessed our lives. At birth, she weighed 7 pounds and 10 ounces, height 19.5 inches. It was a natural birth.

While our baby was perfectly healthy, with charming features, I worried intensely about her somewhat cone-shaped head! And alone in our apartment, I wept a little and prayed to God Almighty for His mercy. However, little did we know about such matters. We soon discovered that the cone-head was due to the tight squeeze for her exit! In the next few days, her head evolved into more natural, normal shape. And once the mother talked about giving a sponge bath to Farah, so I immediately went out and bought some actual sponges!

Good news was sent to all relatives and friends and congratulatory letters are saved in the baby-book. Major events of our daughter's early life are recorded in the baby-book, as also a weekly diary for the first 10 months. We also recorded her sounds for the next several years. Later, as her siblings—Asif and Kashif—came along, we also wrote their weekly diaries and recorded their sounds.

And Rukhsana was soon to graduate and she must attend the convocation for the award of the degree, of course. Our gracious friends, the Saldin family volunteered to take care of our Fari-Pari, while Mom received her degree on Saturday, June 9th. It was uncomfortable to sit on the wooden bench, but Mom had a rubber cushion for her comfort. Of course, Dad was present at the occasion. After the ceremonies, we spent a considerable part of this day with the Saldin family.

2. University of Idaho Faculty Position

While these other developments in our lives occupied us, sometime during 1968, I applied for the immigrant-status visa ("the green-card"). Under the new Federal laws, we were eligible. In due course, we were transferred to this status, and this meant declaration of our intent to eventually become U.S. citizens. The change in status was also desirable for my job search. During spring 1967-68, I was applying for academic positions at various universities and colleges.

Fortunately, I had several offers, effective academic 1968-69, including the neighboring University of Idaho. Since I was still working on my dissertation project and there were some final touches to be completed, we decided to accept the Idaho offer so that I would be close to my committee. The idea was that at least for the academic year 1968-69, we will stay at Idaho and then perhaps move elsewhere.

It was not meant to be. Given my decent teaching and research record, with numerous honors and awards, within a few years I was tenured and promoted—and eventually promoted to the full-professor rank in 1974. Having lived in the area for several years, and the community being small and safe for raising a family, we became quite inclined to stay here. The initial short-time affiliation became a life-long commitment. And, unfortunately, there were also occasional unpleasant reminders in my work environment and in our neighborhood—that we were "aliens," "others," "foreigners," "camel jockeys," and suggestions that we ought to return to our origins.

In any case, back to my story. I completed and successfully defended my doctoral research project during 1968-69. During June 1969, I went through the convocation ceremonies for the award of the doctorate degree. Having come to this stage, I felt I had achieved all my academic goals. And I remembered my younger days when I used to almost despise myself for having completed only high-school (10th grade only). And now, here I was—having achieved the ultimate formal education credentials, the doctorate degree. And of course, those days again haunted me with the memory of my late father. None till then in the entire family clan had gone as far in academics as I had; he would have been so proud.

We were well on our way to living a decent, comfortable

life, with our family of three, with some of the usual creature comforts. Having come this far in the struggles of my life is usually what they call the fulfillment of the "American Dream." This land provided me the opportunities, despite many hurdles, and, thanks Almighty, I diligently benefited from them. While things were not always perfect, for there were also occasional reminders of being the "other," however, overall things worked out wonderfully.

And during late summer 1968, we moved to Moscow, Idaho. For this first year, we decided to rent an apartment, within walking distance to the campus. And we bought a new car, a 1969 Ford Maverick. As the year progressed, we found that as a faculty member, we could temporarily rent a university house for one or two years; we lived there for a couple of years. With my full-time faculty position, we were "rich!" We also had a loan to pay to the hospital where our daughter was born. We assumed "full ownership" of our baby several months after her birth.

However, as it turned out, the area became our life-long home. And in 2002, I took the emeritus-faculty status, but continued teaching on a part-time basis till 2008. And, reluctantly, we moved to Atlanta, Georgia, in May 2013, where our daughter and her family live, as well as the family of my brother-in-law. We are now settled in Acworth, a suburb of Atlanta, Georgia

3. Pakistan Visit, Summer 1969

I remembered my commitment to my father-in-law that we would return to Pakistan after four years—and that meant summer 1969. I also wished to explore the possibility of a job, so we might eventually settle in Pakistan. And, of course, everyone was anxious to see our lovely daughter, now a little over one year old. We went to

Pakistan during summer 1969. En route, we stayed a few days in London, and then on our return, we visited Paris, Amsterdam, and Weisbaden, Germany. In Weisbaden, we visited my friend from undergraduate years, Garry Ratliff and his family; he was stationed at the U.S. Air Force Base there.

The visit to Pakistan and connecting with all our relatives and friends was most satisfying. Of course, the center of attention throughout was our daughter. Further, I explored job prospects in Pakistan; that was commitment with my father-in-law in 1965. However, I was discouraged, and, indeed, several friends asked if I could assist them in moving to the USA! As for my father-in-law, he was satisfied that we were comfortably settled in the USA. His reaction was wise and gracious: "Live wherever you both are happy; after all, it is your life together."

Soon the three of us flew to Karachi, and then returned to the U.S., via Europe, as planned. Once we returned to Moscow, we felt we were in a somewhat different mindset as to our future. The trip to Pakistan had persuaded us to try to settle in the U.S. on a longer-term basis. We decided that we should buy a house of our own. Fortunately, a small 3-bedroom house became available, within walking distance of the campus; we bought this house. As we moved into our house, Rukhsana resumed her part-time studies toward the master's degree. The timings of Rukhsana's schedule worked out just fine and rather compatible with my own teaching schedule. As the mother would go to her classes, sometimes I would stay with our daughter and sometimes she would be in the care of a baby-sitter nearby. Things worked out just wonderfully. And the young mother earned her master's degree in June 1971.

4. The Son Rises!

That expression, of course, is a take from the famous novel, <u>The Sun Also Rises</u>, by late Ernest Hemingway, except for our family, it is our son, our first son, Asif—and his 'rising' was the most blessed event in our lives in 1972 and indeed, the most significant event of my personal life. A son whose father, unlike the father's father, hopes and prays to be around for many, many years of his life. And later, our joys were infinitely multiplied when our second son 'arose'—Kashif, born November 21, 1975.

Perhaps during August 1971, we discovered that my dear wife was pregnant again. Of course, we were anxious to have another child; and having a daughter already, we all prayed for a son—sort of an instinct for most couples, I suppose. Weeks and months progressed rather satisfactorily. And, then the most auspicious day arrived for us, tearfully the most blissful, the most joyous event of my life. We were blessed by God Almighty with a son, yes, the son also rose! Born at 9.34 a.m., Thursday, April 20, 1972, at the Memorial Hospital, Pullman, Asif Ahmed Ghazanfar, weighed 6 pounds and 15 ounces, length 19.25 inches, healthy, handsome, and complete in every way. I named him after my childhood friend, Asif, as an expression of my affection for him. And, as with our daughter, we started a weekly diary for our new born baby also. There are so many, many details in those diaries. In addition to this weekly diary, I also started recording Asif's sounds, just as I had for our daughter, but now often with both. And, over the years, I have often noted in the diaries some important 'firsts' of our children, including major events.

It is common knowledge that I am an emotional softie, but especially so when it comes to our children. Like all infants, Asif also had his usual minor ailments. However, in July 1972, he had a serious health issue—bronchial infection. Medicine caused him to be badly constipated and uncomfortable all night, crying and unable to sleep. I took him to his doctor the next morning; being weak of heart that I was, I asked a friend to accompany. Obviously, he was in intense pain—and it caused me enormous pain to see my little baby suffering. The doctor gave my infant son a suppository to ease constipation—and surely that worked quickly. From Asif's baby-book, July 23:

> "All of this shook up Daddy terribly. He had a tough time seeing me go through all this," as written in the diary. The doctor suggested that my baby-son should be given two injections—one in each thigh. As the nurse began doing the injections, I could not bear to see my son's agony and the pain from the injection and his crying, so I left the room in tears, with our friend attending to my son during those moments. After two-three hours, we came home—and now I just couldn't hold and cried profusely. They love me so very much—so precious to them."

> In the next few days, our son fully recovered.

5.   Pakistan Visit, Fall 1974

Now that I was well-established at the University of Idaho, I was eligible—and I was awarded—sabbatical leave for the academic year 1974-75. I intended to pursue a research project in Pakistan, so we went to Pakistan for the fall semester, 1974. And I planned to spend the spring semester, auditing some courses at the University of Maryland. We drove to New York and left our car with a friend there. And then flew from New York to Pakistan. Now we were visiting with two children, Fari-Pari, 6 years old and Asif, 2 years old. Everyone saw Asif for the first time; he was the star.

Our semester-long stay in Pakistan was most satisfying—professionally as well as personally. With assistance from Punjab University, I conducted a survey for my research project and gathered data, which later led to some publications; also, I gave a few seminars on various topics. We returned to the USA late December 1974. Then we drove to Maryland and I connected with the University of Maryland and audited some courses there. We had intended to rent an apartment on the campus, however, my cousin and his family insisted that we stay with them, which we did. It was a joyful few months with them. Then, about mid-May 1975, we drove back to our University of Idaho campus-community life in late May 1975.

6. Another Son Rises!

During our return journey, my lovely wife at times experienced some nausea and exhaustion—a bit of a mystery that we thought was due to the travel. And soon, the mystery was solved—we happily discovered that our precious second son, Kashif, was on the way! This is when we also decided to buy a larger house, especially since we were soon to be a family of five.

This pregnancy experience for Rukhsana was slightly different. The gynecologist suspected, especially during the last few months, that perhaps we were likely to be blessed with twins. It was not so, however. As the day arrived, and the doctor was helping with the exit, he saw the baby's long eye-lashes and exclaimed, "It is a girl." Then, a few second later, he said, "Sorry—it is a boy!" And we were blessed with another son, Kashif Ahmed Ghazanfar, born on Friday, November 21, 1975, 7 pounds, 5 ounces, height 20 inches. As for my emotional state, again the memory of my father was overwhelming: how ecstatic he would have been to know that he had another grandson from his only son.

And I had my contemplative moments. Having gone through the bleakest circumstances of my lonely childhood and youth, and having patiently absorbed the physical and emotional violence inflicted by the monster of a "step-father," here I was—having achieved some success in my life, well-established professionally, and a wonderful, lovely wife, a happy married life, and three charming children, our most precious joys of life—our daughter and our sons. I am so grateful for all the blessings God Almighty bestowed upon us.

During summer 1980, we traveled to Pakistan again. Now the five of us—and the star now was our youngest, Kashif, almost 5 years old. In fact, over the next several years, we went to Pakistan more than once, especially when we were located in Jeddah, Saudi Arabia. I was invited to serve as a visiting faculty at the King Abdulaziz University, Jeddah, Saudi Arabia, and we lived there for three years, 1983-1986.

Years passed by and I was approaching the final stage of my professional career. I took the emeritus-faculty status from the University of Idaho in 2002, an agonizing moment of my life. The academic career was more than a profession; it was a profoundly satisfying personal journey that enabled me the good fortune of connecting with younger friends— my extended family—whose lives I could, hopefully, influence in positive ways. It was not easy to relinquish my hobby and disconnect with my 'extended' family! In fact, I continued to teach part-time until spring 2008.

My career choice nurtured my mind and soul, and expanded my horizons as a human-being, with holistic, diversified intellectual passions. Simultaneously, I was always keen to "give" back, for I "received" so much in my life; I firmly believe that in the long-run, it all "averages out" just fine.

And there were so many opportunities that gave me the joy of satisfying that intrinsic need—my immediate community, friends, students, and others.

Chapter XIV

MY CAREER, MY COMMUNITY

In the late 1950s when I was pursuing my plans for higher education in the United States, my career aspirations were based mainly on observing others in my surroundings who were well-placed in the business world, earning a substantial income, and living a comfortable life. Once I would complete my bachelor's degree in Business Administration in the United States, I would return to Pakistan and establish myself as a business executive. That kind of professional life was my ideal. My world was rather narrow, as was my mind.

As I pursued higher education in the U.S., my vision broadened, and I found myself gradually gravitating toward more fulfilling career choices. I became aware of other possibilities in my new environment, and while life was a challenge at the time, what seemed possible also seemed attainable, though requiring greater investment of time and effort. And there were opportunities available.

It was when I was taking courses, as an undergraduate, such as marketing, sales-management, and others, I discovered my limitations to be an effective business executive. I could not function in an environment where the ultimate goal was the pursuit of profit-maximization, even when there may be negative social, even unethical, though legally-acceptable, consequences. I began to realize that I would likely be encountering conscience-driven situations of personal conflict. Of course, profit-maximization is the life-blood of our capitalistic economic system and there are entrepreneurs and others who happily function as the driving force of the system. However, as human beings, not all are equipped to perform those functions; I felt I was one of the ill-equipped.

1. My Career Choice

At this time, I made the key choice: I decided to pursue the goal of preparing myself to be a university-level academic faculty. Secondly, I had to decide as to which field. What is great about undergraduate education is one's exposure to different areas of knowledge as part of the curriculum. I was quite drawn to both Economics and Sociology. However, I gathered from my advisors and others that Economics would offer more professional opportunities, domestic as well as global, compared to Sociology. Thus, I decided that I would pursue graduate education in Economics. I was confident that I would be admitted in the graduate school to pursue the doctorate degree, with financial assistance. It was a longer-term goal, more challenging than the bachelor's degree, but certainly well worth it. I earned my master's in Economics in 1964 and doctorate in 1968. My inclination to be an academic professional strengthened as I progressed. Teaching profession, I believed, would enable one to impart learning as well as to import learning in the process. I decided to follow the same profession as my late father's.

Among the various options available, I chose to join the University of Idaho, effective Fall 1968. Initially I thought it would be temporary till we move elsewhere. However, that became a life-long commitment.

2. Professional Life/Recognitions

From the very outset, I felt committed to the academic life, teaching, research, and service being the professional responsibilities. Once I was immersed in the system, each aspect of the profession became a pleasure to pursue and I tried to accomplish my obligations as best as I possibly could. Support for that statement comes from the fact that throughout each year of my 35-years long academic career, I was fortunate to be rated "excellent/excellent-plus" in annual performance reviews.

Guided by my conviction that students must be accorded all the opportunities to succeed, I always volunteered to be available on call ("24-hours daily"), and to meet them about anywhere of their convenience—and often I did so. I always invited my top students for lunch; and even took the weak students for lunch so I could encourage and guide. Further, numerous students earned their master's (and some doctorate) degrees under my supervision. Many are well-placed professionals around the country and abroad.

My research productivity was often the envy of my colleagues—at least one or more professional publications annually (and continuing!), a total of over 170 thus far, as well as four well-received books. My research portfolio has been quite diversified—public finance, taxation issues, global development issues, history of economic thought, Islam-West civilizational linkages, etc. Several of these publications have been internationally recognized and I continue to receive occasional comments and inquiries about various topics, including invitations to keynote and/or participate in conferences abroad. In addition, I played key service roles in the state, the most prominent being service to the Idaho Legislature as a budget-consultant for 24 years. Further, often I volunteered to transport students to or from the airport, in addition to often hosting foreign students in our house for a few days and even for several semesters. I am fortunate to be occasionally in contact with numerous students, even in retirement.

For my professional accomplishments, I was blessed with numerous performance honors and awards, some student-initiated, others emanating from the university administration (often naming me a "legend"): three university-wide distinguished/outstanding faculty awards, twenty alumni-excellence faculty awards, alumni-excellence award for life-time contributions, the Hall of Fame/Pride-of-Pakistan Award (London) in 1983, etc. Thankfully, I am listed in numerous recognition-listings, such as Who's Who (regional, national, international), International Biography (London), Men of Achievement, American Registry of Outstanding Professionals, 500 Leaders of Influence, and several others. During the 1990s, the University of Idaho established the "Ghazi Seminar Room" in the privately-funded College building, supported by $100,000 contributed by my former students. And the University has established a "Ghazanfar Endowment Fund" to generate scholarships for undergraduate students.

And in 2009, the University of Idaho honored me with the highly-coveted "Idaho Treasure Award." And "in recognition of valuable contributions to Unity," the University awarded me the 2013 Unity Service Medallion. Further, based on my overall professional activities, my alma-mater, Washington State University honored me with the Distinguished Alumni Achievement Award in 2007. In that year, my alma-mater also inducted me in the University's Hall of Honored Alumni.

3. Community Involvement

Once I was fairly well established professionally, I looked for opportunities to contribute in some meaningful ways to the larger community. I volunteered to provide transportation to senior citizens, or join them for conversations at the senior center, and for years I participated in the community's "meals-on-wheels" program. It was indeed an expression of my keen desire to "give" back, for I "received" so much in life; and such experiences have always been so comforting for the soul.

There were numerous other activities that personally enhanced the quality of my life.

Decades ago, I helped to establish an Interfaith Council in the community to promote understanding about each other's faith affiliation, though some denominations refused to join. Further, I initiated a once-a-semester interfaith picnic. My passions also included participation in human-rights activities in the area; I was one of the founding-members of the local Human-Rights Task Force. Later, I was one of the founding-members of the City-Hall's Human Rights Commission. These groups continue to be active.

In 2005, I initiated what became known as the annual CommUNITY Walk, the sole objective being the promotion of "Unity within Diversity." Several like-minded community friends joined the venture. The activity was formally recognized by the City Hall, the Governor of Idaho and the Idaho Legislature. Each year, the volunteer-group raised several thousand dollars from the community business and individuals for the day's activities. Several hundred community members gathered in the city center on the last

Saturday of each April, held some festive activities there, and then carrying suitable banners and flyers, everyone, chanting and singing, walked to the city park where more festive activities took place, reflecting the theme of the event. Then followed a luncheon for all participants. The Walk continued for the next ten years and is enshrined in the inclusive history of the community.

For all such pursuits, the community has been most kind in acknowledging my contributions. For my "Caring and Serving" contributions, I am recognized in the <u>Legendary Locals of Moscow, Idaho</u>, published by the Latah County Historical Society, Moscow, Idaho (2015). Over the years, I have been honored with several awards—the Martin Luther King Award, the Human-Rights Commission Award, and the Unity Award. And in 2013, the community established a bench in the name of my wife and I at the city park. And there is a tree planted in my honor in that park.

Given my lowly origins, I can humbly state that I am truly a most blessed human-being—thanks Almighty.

But, as I was approaching my formal disconnect, my emeritus status, from my academic career, there remained the pursuit of another, most somber wish of my life—my desire to go back to my roots, where it all began, my birth-place in India, where I lost my father, and where the traumas of my childhood began. Invitations to present professional papers in Europe and India provided the opportunity.

And I took that sentimental journey in February 2000.

Chapter XV

SENTIMENTAL JOURNEY TO MY ROOTS, PART I

And, here I am now, concluding this odyssey with a narrative on my sentimental journey to the place of my birth, my roots, my childhood—Phillaur, East Punjab, India. This was the place where I was born in 1937, where my father met his pre-mature demise, where the murderer of my father entered our lives as "step-father," where I experienced so many cruelties and traumas of my early life, and where also began the miseries of our family life. This is where I sometimes starved—and also, starved for my childhood, yet hungry for life, where adversities seemed endless and my struggles were between despair and hope.

Additionally, however, I was also captured by the *zeitgeist* of a generation: so many survivors of partition were seizing a last chance to reconcile their contradictory memories of terrorized displacement, but also of a rich shared culture that had to be left behind. The sacred journey was the ultimate yearning throughout my life, and finally, it became possible, almost 53 years after our migration in late August 1947. An intensely emotional experience, I experienced several tearful outbursts on so many occasions. I visited and walked through every nook and corner of the house where I was born, lived—and survived—my early life, and where I could viscerally experience the dreadful moments of my childhood. I traveled to seek some spiritual solace and closure for the suffering of my early life. In retrospect, however, I must acknowledge, closure has not been possible. Memories linger on and the pain stubbornly persists and survives; there is no escaping.

1. Planning the Journey

Before going on this mission, I first had to explore various avenues to ensure that there were meaningful connections in Phillaur. First, I found someone in Illinois who had once attended the same school in Phillaur where my late father taught and where I completed my fifth grade. This gentleman volunteered to connect me with his cousin in Ludhiana (a city, about 10 miles from Phillaur)—Manjeet Singh Grewal, who attended the same high school and whose father was once the principal of Phillaur High School. I established connection with him; and I found him to be a supremely wonderful man to know.

Later, I sent a letter to the Principal of Phillaur High School, not knowing him personally but I felt confident that in a small town, perhaps still with only one high school, the letter would reach him; and fortunately, it did. My letter provided details of why I wished to visit Phillaur, along with a detailed map I developed from my memory—how I would walk through various meandering streets, from our house to the high school; I also identified some key places along the way to school—the local open market, the mosques, the temples, etc.

Soon I received a most cordial response from the Principal, Mr. Prem Kumar. He was eager to welcome me.

Later, I also inquired of him if two Hindu friends from my childhood—who were also my father's students—still lived in the area. I was informed that one of them had passed away and the other, Jawahar Lal (6-7 years older than me), whose family lived opposite our house, was a well-established businessman in the area. When informed of my planned visit, he was anxious to see me and welcome me. Such positive developments persuaded me to further solidify my travel plans. In anticipation, I had already obtained the visa to travel to India. In the meantime, I had received an invitation to present a seminar at the Aligarh University, Aligarh, India. Further, I had committed to present a paper at a professional conference in Graz, Austria, late February, during my return travel.

Also, I had earlier alerted a friend (a former student at my alma mater, Washington State University) in New Delhi who was keen to assist and facilitate my travels in India. Another friend from India linked me to her brother in Jullundur (East Punjab, India), about 35 miles from Phillaur. I wished to visit this city also, where many relatives lived before India's partition and where my wife was born. And this was the city to which I ran away twice to escape the wrath of the "step-father."

2. The Journey

All plans finalized, and after a few days in Pakistan, I landed in New Delhi on February 7, 2000. This in itself was an emotional experience, for this was the land of my birth, with so much history of a rather amicable coexistence of various religious groups. We migrated from India in August 1947 when I was 10 years old and now I was here 53 years later. My host-friend met me at the airport and took me to his house where I rested for a couple of days and then embarked on my primary mission.

Of course, I was a bit concerned about where I would stay in Phillaur. How I wound get around, who would assist me to visit the various places in my town, and also, there was concern about any health hazards, etc. Happily, these concerns were resolved through the courtesy of my host's relative who came to see me for a friendly connection. He volunteered to put me in touch with his friend in Phillaur, who was the Director of Punjab Police Academy, a rather prominent position. I was told that he would take care of all the logistics of my stay in Phillaur. That was a small miracle, absolutely unexpected; everything worked out most satisfactorily.

Soon after my arrival, I contacted Manjeet Grewal in Ludhiana (a city near Phillaur). He was genuinely anxious to welcome me. Having not met him before, he gave some details about his identity. Then I called Prem Kumar, the Principal of Phillaur High School; he too expressed enthusiasm about my visit; I told him my approximate arrival date. My host was kind enough to arrange all my travel plans—by train to Phillaur and then, later, in a rented car to Aligarh.

3.   Train to Phillaur

On February 9th, I took the train to Ludhiana where Manjeet had planned to meet me at the train depot, and then I would go to Phillaur. I had given him the identity of my train-compartment. The compartment was rather stuffy—a bit crowded, warm weather, and non-functional air-conditioner, yet fairly comfortable; interactions with passengers around me were interesting. Along the route, the train stopped at several cities which I could recall from

Indian history as centers of historic battles—Sonapat, Panipat, Ambala, etc.

As the train stopped at the Ludhiana depot, I could see Manjeet, standing in front of my compartment—in his maroon turban and necktie. I got off the train and we both instinctively walked toward each other, as though we have known each other for ages, and with tears rolling down our eyes, we embraced each other. There was intense mutuality of our emotions, evoked by the consciousness of our roots. Hardly any words expressed, but we hugged each other again and again. And then, still with tears in his eyes, he recited a very touching verse from a famous poet. In English translation, it was: "I meet a friend and there is a pleasant glow on my face; but he thinks I was ill and my ailment is now alleviated!" We shed some more tears.

Manjeet was overwhelmed, for he was meeting someone who was once from the "other" side of India. He and his family had migrated in 1947 from Sialkot, now part of Pakistan, and where one of his young sisters had died and was buried. I was overwhelmed, not only because I was connecting with such a warm human being, but also because here I was—after several decades, on the soil of my roots, from which I disconnected under harsh conditions in 1947. Both of our families were once refugees, on each side of the divided sub-continent. I found out he was now a retired Indian government official.

4. Meeting a Childhood Friend

As we walked on the platform toward the exit gate, Manjeet was talking about the surroundings of the train depot. Filled with emotions, I impulsively bent down and kissed the ground. Then, I saw a person not far from us and looking at my behavior. He asked me, "Sir, have you come from abroad?" I said, "yes, I am here to visit my birth-place in Phillaur." He was also from Phillaur, he said. I mentioned the name of my friend, Jawahar Lal. He somehow had some inkling and said, "Sir, his clothing store is not far from here and he is waiting for you." Small world. He gave us directions and Manjeet and I headed toward that store—Paris Cloth House.

Soon we found the store. And there he was—my childhood friend from our neighborhood's Hindu family, my late father's student—Jawahar Lal. We were meeting after 53 years; I was about 10 and he about 16 when we last saw each other in 1947. There was such exuberance of emotions and joy. He was standing there with open arms and we embraced, with our eyes moist. We readily recognized each other; he told me I looked about the same as when he last saw me. He was a well-established businessman, with operations also in England.

Manjeet and I sat with Jawahar for a while; he pointed to the picture of his late father on the wall. We were entertained with cold drinks and snacks. He invited me to stay with him. We talked about our families and I briefly stated the trials and tribulations of my life. He mentioned that our mothers used to be good friends and that my elder sister used to teach him mathematics. He mentioned that once he slapped another elder sister of mine—and then his mother ensured that she must slap him back—and she did. He talked of his marriage with a Christian girl, opposed by parents, but resolved by the blessings that he received from praying at the shrine of a Muslim saint, located in the local fort. He mentioned that many Hindus and Sikhs go to this shrine every Thursday and pray to receive blessings. He also mentioned that the mosque in the neighborhood was now a Sikh temple.

Jawahar Lal, of course, knew everyone in the neighborhood from the early days. There were others in the neighborhood who knew my father and our family, some who were also my father's students. He talked highly of my father—a fine gentleman, a simple man, with roundish face. For his gentle, relaxed mannerism, everyone called him "Baadshao" (the 'kingly' man). Jawahar knew about the murder—and the murderer—of my father. He mentioned that my father's relatives wanted the body exhumed for police action, but the issue was suppressed to minimize the scandal. Even the monster's wife wanted the body exhumed and pressed charges against her murderer-husband.

The most painful news that Jawahar Lal conveyed was the fact that the graveyard where my father and two sisters were buried existed no more; all graves were washed away when floods happened some years ago. My father's grave had always been so vivid in my memory and I was keenly looking forward to going there, remember him, tell him how much I have missed him all my life, and say prayers; but no more. I wept from hearing this news.

5. Visit to My School

I told Jawahar that I was committed to visit my school in Phillaur and meet Prem Kumar, the Principal that afternoon, February 9th. He suggested that he would arrange for me to come to his Phillaur house next day so that I could visit 'my' birth-place house and the neighborhood. He introduced me to his son, Mukesh ("Mickey"), who was visiting from England. Jawahar Lal asked his son to drive me to the school, about 15 miles away. Accompanied by Manjeet, we headed for Phillaur and went directly to the school. As we entered the city, the streets seemed so familiar, as was the forest on the opposite side of the school structure. We approached the school—and there was the familiar semi-circular sign above the main entry-gate: Phillaur High School. I was 10 years old at the time, but the memories are always fresh—and come alive in a flash.

As we entered the school grounds, there was another entry-gate—and there was Prem Kumar, the Principal, and the entire school staff (about 15-16 of them, including some ladies), standing there to welcome me. I warmly hugged and shook hands with everyone and also met the ladies appropriately. And it was a most touching welcome; Prem Kumar handed me a bouquet of flowers. Of course, I was emotional. I could see my late father walking on those grounds. I could see myself on these grounds as a young student. I could see myself standing in the morning exercise drill—and then quietly running away from there, twice, to catch the train to Jullundhar to escape from "step-father's" hell-house and his clutches.

Then we entered the school grounds proper—rectangular structure, with classrooms and administrative offices all around and in the middle of the ground, a cluster of trees, surrounded with flower plants. We walked in front of the classrooms; and I saw slab on the wall that said the school was established in 1926. As we reached the room at the northwest corner, I was told it was the school library; there were some lady staff members and I exchanged greetings with them, which they shyly acknowledged, and they allowed me to take a picture. However, I remembered this room as the 'arts classroom,' where, according to Jawahar Lal, my father used to teach arts and where, I recalled, I too sat as a 5th-grade student. Prem Kumar told me that, indeed, this room once was the 'arts classroom.'

6. My Father's Traces

We ended up in the Principal's Office, where several staff members were awaiting to welcome me. Prem Kumar introduced me to each of them. After exchanging some pleasantries and sharing the memories of my younger days in the city, I mentioned that I was too young when my father passed away and I do not even know what he looked like; there were no pictures anywhere. In fact, I have no tangible remnant about his life. Then, I inquired if there were any group pictures of school teachers from previous years, where there might be a picture of my late father. The answer, as I expected, was negative.

Then I inquired about any school records where I could my father's hand-writing. Prem Kumar mentioned that there were stacks of year-by-year file-folders, going back several decades, which were stored in several steel almirahs; and there might be some such document. My father passed away in March 1941, so, I asked, if we could browse through some folders for a few years prior to 1941. That became the project for several of us, each browsing through the year-by-year folders and searching for the writing of my father in some form—an application for leave, a request for some school supplies, a note concerning a student, etc.

Then one of the staff members pointed to a signature and exclaimed, "Sir, is this your father's name?" "Yes, yes….. yes, indeed; Sheikh Mehboob Bakhsh. That is his name and his signature," I screamed out crying; my excitement was explosive. I hugged the young man who discovered the signature. What a blessed discovery—as though I found something that was lost all through my life; I was ecstatic; I was, at last, looking at his writing, looking at the paper touched by my father's hands. The name and signature were discovered on a payroll-roster page for the month of May

1939 that listed the names of all school teachers, along with monthly salary, some deductions, net salary, followed by the signature of the teacher in the last column. The signature indicated receipt of the salary.

Obviously, one discovery led to other similar documents for other months and years.

And I did see several, with my father's name and signature—some I left behind with traces of my tears on them. And, I wanted copies of a few of those roster-pages; Prem Kumar, the Principal, was kind enough to oblige. I also asked for one or two original pages. Prem Kumar hesitated, for those were historic documents. However, I convinced him that none is ever likely to come again with this request—and that the original may be replaced with a copy. He agreed, and I deeply appreciated that he gave me a couple of originals. Those are my treasures now.

I mentioned to Prem Kumar that a New Delhi acquaintance was a good friend of the Director of the Punjab Police Academy and he had contacted the Director about my stay at the Academy Officers' Mess. Prem Kumar called the Director's Office and soon I was sitting with the Director, Mr. Abdul Ahad Siddiqui, a highly-decorated official, who welcomed me warmly. I told him why I was visiting here. He gave instructions to his assistant, Rakesh Bharati, about my stay at the Academy. In the interim, Prem Kumar and Manjeet were sitting in the assistant's office. Incidentally, everyone was so surprised that, even after decades of living in the West, I could still fluently converse in the local Punjabi language.

7. Stay at VIP Guest House

Accompanied by Rakesh, we arrived at the Academy Officers Mess, also called the Government Guest House. Also accompanying me were Manjeet and Prem Kumar. As we entered its long driveway, a flood of memories flashed back; I pensively stood with tears in my eyes and everyone wondered. And I explained. This was the same driveway from where, late August 1947, our bus-caravan, with protective armed jeeps in front and back, each bus packed with refugees, including our family, departed for the arduous journey to Pakistan's border, 90 miles away, with the uncertainty whether we would reach there alive or not. Of course, much of India and Pakistan was engulfed in riotous conditions at the time. Someone from our neighborhood worked as a cook for the British and he was instrumental in working with the British in arranging this bus-caravan for our migration

What an irony of fate—here I was, 53 years later, honored to stay in this VIP Guest House, where, I was told, India's Prime Minister, late Indira Gandhi, late Yasser Arafat of the Palestine Liberation Organization, and other dignitaries had stayed. The entire complex was once part of the British-operated Police Training Center, now called Punjab Policy Academy, and the Britishers used to stay in these quarters.

There were several Guest House employees who welcomed me. I was escorted to the quarters where I would stay the next few days. The place was excellent, with all the comforts that one would find in any fine hotel. There were helpers/aides all around for my convenience and, as per the

Academy's protocol, an armed guard at the door! Soon an aide brought tea and refreshments for us. It was getting a bit late. Manjeet, Prem Kumar, and Rakesh left for the evening; they planned to return next morning. This day, February 9th, was indeed a busy day—traveling from New Delhi to Ludhiana, meeting Manjeet Singh, connecting with old friend, Jawahar Lal, meeting the Academy Director and arriving at the Academy Guest House for my stay, visiting the Phillaur school where my late father taught and where, much later, I was a student, and, most importantly, *discovering the signature of my late father.* Also, I met the Academy's Deputy Director, Chandar Shekhar, who was staying in the adjacent room. He was very friendly and keen to do whatever was needed for my comfort. Indeed, a most memorable day but somewhat exhaustive. And, there is so much more to come.

8. Visiting My Birth-Place

Next day, February 10th, I woke up around 7 a.m. I took a shower and got ready for the day's activities. And then breakfast arrived; the aide would obediently stand in the room in case I needed any other service from him— my clothes ironed, my shoes polished, etc.; it was a bit embarrassing for someone who was so accustomed to being quite independent about such matters. Then Manjeet, Prem Kumar, and Rakesh arrived.

And then began the most momentous day of my visit to India.

As planned, Jawahar Lal's son, Mukesh, arrived to bring me to the area of my childhood house and my old memories; of course, Jawahar Lal's house was also in the same neighborhood. We arrived there and Jawahar Lal was waiting for me. And it was like a nightmarish, though comforting, dream—the streets of my childhood—what agony, what ecstasy. We walked to *my* street—the street where I could see my mother being kicked out of the house by the abusive monster, the "step-father." As we were walking, Jawahar Lal mentioned that our mothers were friends and often his mother intervened to save us from the monster's violence.

And then there was *the* house, the house of my birth, the spaces where I endured and suffered so much, as did my mother and my sisters. The house had the same basic structure as when we lived there, but substantially upgraded—modern appliances, newer doors and windows, etc. The present residents of the house welcomed me warmly. As I entered the house, I was quite distraught in my emotional condition and I had to explain why. I was in the room, now the living room where sofas were arranged in one corner. And there, in that corner, I could see the dead body of my murdered father laid on a bed, with a wrap around his face and head. And I could see myself, the almost 4-years old child, standing near the bed, crying and sobbing. And now, at age 63, I was standing at about the same spot—and once again, crying and sobbing, weeping uncontrollably. I was absolutely drenched; Jawahar Lal understood my condition and he tried to console me. And I was explaining to those around me what I could see, and they couldn't; they understood.

Then I walked to the exit-room of the house (this opened to the street)—and there I could see a goat tied to a peg in this room, the one, as a youngster, I used to walk to the farms for grazing. This was the room from which I could see my mother being dragged, beaten, kicked, and pushed out to the street by the monster. Then there was the courtyard of the house where I could see my mother sitting on a floor-mat, sewing clothes for neighbors to earn some money for the family—and I am sitting nearby, leaned toward my mother, and waiting for her to ask me to thread the needle.

And, on one side of the courtyard, there used to be a curtain-drawn bathroom where we used to take baths from water-buckets. On the other side of this open area was the earthen-oven, where, on wooden fire, mother would cook food and we would sit nearby on the floor to eat. This was also the area where I would run around from corner to corner, screaming and trying to escape from the beatings of the monster, as he chased me with a stick or shoe. Sometimes I would be pushed to the concrete wall and I would be injured; there are scars.

Then there was that room, the larger room, now split in two. And this was the room where I could remember so much abuse that I suffered, as did my mother and sisters. And, indeed, this was the room of my most traumatized memories. That was when I ran away, twice, to escape by train to Jullundhur. There was that door in the middle that led to another room in the back. It was the upper ledge of this door where there was a metal hook to which, with my hands tied, I used to be hung; and then mercilessly beaten by the monster. As an 8-9 years old lad, sometimes I would feel as though he was going to choke me, and I would die; for he knew I was a witness to some of his beastly deeds. My mother and sisters, crying and wailing, would try to intervene, but then they too would suffer the monster's wrath. Now, decades later, I was holding that ledge of the door; crying from the painful memories, I stood there briefly, reliving my childhood. My hosts understood why. I walked around the room.

And there was that bed where the monster would be lying and I would be massaging his legs and shoulders with my nimble fingers; or he would be sleeping in the summer heat and I would be comforting him by the air generated by the movement of a hand-held, bamboo-stick fan. I could see his shoes under the bed; I was the usual shoe-polisher for him. And that bed also evoked other painful memories. I walked through every nook and corner of the house; I felt as though I was seeking closure and also leaving part of my soul there.

Then I went upstairs and walked around the roof of the house. It was a concrete roof now, compared to the dirt roof when we lived here. That's where we used to sleep during the summers. The surrounding neighborhood structures looked about the same as before—some single-storied, others double or triple-storied, some with more elegant appearance, etc. Around the corner, I saw the dome of a mosque, now converted into a Sikh *gurdawara* (prayer-house).

I profusely thanked my hosts; they were most gracious in putting up with my occasional emotional outbursts. Then I stepped out of the house and my friends—Jawahar Lal, Prem Kumar, and Manjeet—were waiting for me. We walked around the neighborhood and I was able to recall who used to live where—and Jawahar Lal confirmed.

Then I saw the small open area, in front of Jawahar Lal's house, where children used to play with marbles. I recalled I was usually unable to join, for I didn't have any marbles; I would just watch other children play. Sometimes I would ask other children to let me join, pleading "look, I am orphan, I am fatherless; I don't have any marbles." On the roof of this house, Jawahar Lal and other used to fly kites; and I would be there just watching and hoping that someone would momentarily let me hold the string of the flying kite; often my role was to simply hold the reel from which the string would unroll for the kite to fly.

9. Father's Gravesite

I wanted to go to the old graveyard site, where my father and two sisters were once buried. Earlier, I had learned from Jawahar Lal that the graveyard was obliterated some years ago due to flooding from the adjacent River Sutlej; yet I wanted to go there. Jawahar Lal's driver took me there. And there I was looking at houses and other structures built over the land that once was a graveyard. Only grave there was that of Muslim saint, protected with surrounding green-color walls, and green flag in one corner; apparently, it was a site revered even by the local non-Muslims.

There were farms on one side—and the general area where I used to bring the monster's goat for grazing. I stood there in the area for a while where I thought were once the graves of my father and sisters. I wanted to tell my father the trials and tribulations that his only son had suffered throughout, the successes he had achieved with his memory and inspiration, and his wonderful wife and children, his grandchildren whom he would have loved to hold and hug. And I said prayers for his soul, crying and sobbing. The Sikh and Hindu farmers nearby saw me and looked curious. I exchanged greetings with them and explained; and they warmly hugged me.

10. Drive/Walk Around Town

I returned to the neighborhood where my friends were waiting for me. I requested Jawahar Lal if his driver (Sonu) could drive me around town—the streets of my childhood. I parted company and then followed this mission. Manjeet told me he would later come to meet me at the Guest House.

I guided Sonu to the streets I wanted to visit. There was the street that I used to walk to go to my school. Along the way, there was the house of the family to which I often ran to seek help when the monster was abusing my mother. And then, further down, there was the mosque that looked familiar. I found out this mosque was functional and some Muslims (including Mr. Siddiqui, the Director of the Punjab Police Academy) in town come there for prayers. I went in, met the Imam, and said prayers. Next to the mosque, there was the building where there used to be a "dawakhana" (a clinic that practiced in traditional medicines). And then the street meandered toward my school. I didn't go that direction, but I asked Sonu to take me to the center of town—the spots to which I used to walk to buy foodstuffs and other provisions for the household.

The car could not go through the narrow streets, so I decided to walk and told Sonu to meet me on the other side near the Phillaur Railway Station; we both knew exactly what we were talking about. I walked the narrow streets and arrived at the open area of the local markets where farmers would bring their produce to sell; it all looked so familiar. There were some of the familiar shops—the dairy-supplies shops, the fruit-vegetable shops, small department stores, clothing shops, etc. I slowly walked through the area, observing and absorbing—and reliving my childhood days.

Soon I ended up on the other side where there was the famous grand-trunk road that was constructed by the British and linked Peshawar to Calcutta on the western side of colonial India. And in front of me was the Phillaur Railway Station; that's where I went twice, running away from my school, and secretly boarded the train to escape to Jullundhur' and then brought back and punished.

And Sonu was waiting for me and we were driving toward the Guest House. Along the way, I was surprised to see a 'halal' ('kosher') meat shop; I asked Sonu to stop so I could visit the shop. I found out that not only there were

Muslims who would sponsor his shop, but, I was surprised to learn, there were also some Sikh customers.

I returned to the Guest House and rested a bit, reminiscing and absorbing the most memorable moments that experienced today. Soon, a kitchen worker came and politely told me that dinner would be served in my room. Feeling a bit uneasy for such service, I suggested I would rather come to the mess-hall and have dinner there. I went there and enjoyed the dinner and I mingled and chatted with the kitchen workers. Then, Manjeet and I returned to my room. Manjeet recited some Urdu poetry again. He asked that I must somehow find time to briefly visit his house in Ludhiana; I agreed.

Later, Rakesh Bharati came to visit. He talked a bit about his Hindu faith and spirituality.

He mentioned that there is always a religious service nearby on Sundays; perhaps I would like to go. My curiosity was aroused; yes, I would like to go.

It wasn't just a busy day; it was also an emotionally exhaustive day—reliving painful memories of my childhood at every step, seeking closure (though in vain), and absorbing new memories.

11. Homage to the Muslim Saint

Earlier I was told of a highly-revered tomb of an historic Muslim saint, Pir Abdullah Shah, located in the nearby Phillaur Fort; I vaguely remembered hearing about this saint during my childhood. And I was keen to visit and pay homage. I learned that every Friday, throngs of people, almost all non-Muslims, visit the monument, to pay respects, and pray for fulfillment of their noble wishes. To be noted, however, many Muslims would consider such prayers as innovation and heresy.

Briefly, who was this saint? The story is inscribed on a wall near the entrance. Legend has it that when the Sikh rulers of the region, almost 200 years ago, were building the Phillaur Fort, something rather unusual used to happen. Walls would be constructed during the day and next morning they would collapse. Then a religious man had a vision which revealed that if a first born Muslim male, who was also an orphan, be buried alive and then wall be built around him, the walls would not collapse. A pious Muslim mother offered her orphan son as a sacrifice. And then the walls survived, and the fort was built. Ever since, the buried individual, now known as Pir Abdullah Shah, is revered as a saintly figure. Later, the tomb was built in his honor; and Pir Abdullah Shah had many followers in the neighboring areas. Even my childhood friend, Jawahar Lal, was a believer; he told me that years ago, his Hindu parents were not agreeable to his marrying the Christian girl he loved. But, then, he told me, Jawahar Lal used to go to the sacred tomb and prayed; and finally, his parents agreed to the marriage.

As planned, on Friday morning, February 11th, Rakesh Bharati came to take me to the tomb, which was within walking distance. It was raining hard and we had umbrellas. As we stepped outside the Guest House, I was surprised to see a multitude of well-groomed people, most of them non-Muslims, heading toward the sacred place, walking in the rain, with or without umbrellas, others arriving on bicycles or horse-carriages. We walked to the tomb and, as the occasion required, we took our shoes off. Given the large crowd, we had to struggle a bit to get in. There was the grave of the saint, covered with green sheet, surrounded by ritualistic symbols, and fragrance of incense all around. And the visitors, almost all non-Muslims, were faithfully touching and kissing the Muslim saint's grave, quietly whispering prayers. And I wondered—who knows if the intentions are noble, any human being may pray to any sacred figure, Muslim or non-Muslim, or whatever the chosen deity, and be comforted and rewarded accordingly. I stood near the grave and prayed to God Almighty for His blessings. It was a unique and moving experience, indeed.

As scheduled earlier, now I was headed to the Phillaur High School. Jawahar Lal had kindly made his car available for the day.

12. Welcome Reception at School

At the school, Principal Prem Kumar welcomed me and we sat in his office, along with some of his faculty, and we cordially interacted about my early life, my life in the U.S., and my days in town so far. We walked around the school campus—the same grounds where my late father used to walk.

Then I learned that Prem Kumar had arranged a welcome-reception in my honor.

As we approached the reception hall, I noticed almost all faculty and staff were present, including several ladies, who sat separate from men. Prem Kumar introduced me and the audience welcomed me profusely. As planned, I gave a brief talk about my background and my visit. It was an emotional recounting and I was warmly acknowledged. Among other things, I was asked if we—Muslims, Hindus, Sikhs—would ever live together again, as before the 1947 partition. My response was that while I too share those wishes, however, such matters were beyond my control. Then I mingled informally with those present and shared refreshments.

I found that a reporter from the local newspaper was also present for the occasion; he interviewed me and sent me the published story later.

Following the reception, as planned, Sonu came to drive me to his boss's house; Jawahar Lal wanted me to meet some others in the neighborhood who knew my family and some who were my father's students. I also thought of my commitment with Manjeet Grewal that I would visit his house in the evening.

We headed to the neighborhood and there I found Jawahar Lal waiting for me along with another individual, Manohar Lal Bithal. He met me warmly and I found he too was once my father's student. I also met some others in the area. Then we walked around for a while and I absorbed the sights as much as I could. Everything looked about the same as I remembered from my childhood days, except the residents were different.

Then Jawahar Lal's driver took me to Ludhiana to visit the Manjeet Grewal family. Manjeet was gratified to have me in his house, as was his family. His wife and children gathered in the living room to interact with me. Manjeet recited some Urdu poetry and mentioned that the younger generation had no appreciation of Urdu poetry. He also quietly shared his agony, in that his sons refuse to wear the traditional Sikh-religion turban.

We parted company after an hour or so; and it was an emotional farewell, for I didn't expect to see him again soon. Next day I had planned to go to Jullundhur and then, the following day, I was scheduled to return to New Delhi. Manjeet and I promised to stay in touch; and we did for the next few years, till his passing away in 2005.

It was indeed a hectic but a very enjoyable day. I returned to the Guest House. Next day was to be another memorable day: visit to our ancestral city—and the city of my childhood experiences, Jullundhur.

Chapter XVI

SENTIMENTAL JOURNEY TO MY ROOTS, PART II

These last few days were most unique and memorable, distinctly different in so many ways from any other period of my life. The sentimental journey continues, however.

And Friday, February 12ᵗʰ, the visit to Jullundhur where too are embedded so many childhood memories. With assistance from Chander Shekhar, the Deputy Director of the Academy, arrangements had been made for an Academy vehicle to drive me to Jullundhur.

Chander Shekhar called me, from his Chandigarh residence (about 30 miles away), to ensure if all arrangements were satisfactory and to invite me to join him in an afternoon wedding reception at a Ludhiana hotel that same day.

At about 11 a.m., the Academy van arrived, with driver, Sukhwinder Singh, and consistent with the protocol, an armed guard, Gurmit Singh, to take me to Jullundhur, about 35 miles away, in a police van. I had earlier established contact with a close friend's brother, Jagjeet Singh, in Jullundhur, who had promised to facilitate the visit. I had informed him of the city's general area where several of our relatives lived before partition; it was called "Rasta Mohalla."

1. Drive to Jullundhur

As we drove to Jullundhur, names of some small towns along the highway seemed familiar, as was the general surrounding area. We went directly to Jagjeet's house and this area looked quite new and unfamiliar; he and his family welcomed me warmly. Jagjeet had already linked with a fine individual who lived in the Rasta Mahalla area—Mr. Kundan Lal Sharma, General Manager of the local daily newspaper, <u>Veer-Partaap</u>, published in Urdu and Punjabi languages. We went to his office; I found him to be very cordial individual, generous in spirit and in his humanity. He and his family had migrated from Gujrat, Pakistan; and he had gone back there some years ago and he understood the purpose of my visit. Accompanied by Kundan Lal, we drove to the Rasta Mohalla area. My escorts parked the van there.

The three of us—Kundan Lal, Jagjeet, and I—walked through the streets of Rasta Mahalla. There had been many changes, it seemed; some streets/structures seemed familiar; others were not. But we walked around in the hope that I would see some familiar spot. And suddenly I did—the old "family haveli," the huge, historic mansion-like structure that was built by the larger family clan, perhaps more than a century ago. I recognized the huge entry-door, with a window above. Once or twice, I recalled, I briefly lived in a room of this mansion, with my mother and the "step-father;" why that stay—I have no idea. I understood that the entire structure was being demolished, to be replaced with a shopping mall. Then I recalled there used to be a mosque in the street behind. We walked there and discovered the mosque, now a Hindu temple; and further down, there was an area called "panj-peer" ("five-saints"). Now I was thinking of some other relatives' houses in reference to this structure. We walked around and then I spotted the house where one of my uncle (eldest brother of mother) used to live. However, we were unsuccessful in finding the house of my aunt where I used to come as a run-away child.

2. Interfaith Lunch

And now a most unusual, gratifying experience. Kundal Lal invited me to have lunch in his house. Jagjeet and I accompanied him. His wife had prepared a delicious meal for us. And the most fascinating aspect of this event was this. Here were three human-beings—a Muslim, a Hindu Brahman, and a Sikh—sharing food together. It was a most generous gesture on the part of Kundan Lal family, which I deeply appreciated. And most unusual; ordinarily, orthodox individuals of the three faiths would not sit with the other to share food, not even touch any utensils of the "other." This was a most touching experience. Some won't even eat food, nor drink water, from a utensil that was earlier used by one from the other faith. And that hideous practice still prevails among many.

3. Escape-House Discovered

And then a remarkable thing happened as we were walking toward the parked van.

I noticed a gated entrance, with a couple of stairs, to a large house and that, I recalled, where some distant relatives lived. And now I knew my aunt's house was on the back of this house. So, we turned around. And there it was—the house of my escapes, the house of my aunt, exactly as I remembered. This was also the house where, I recalled, my mother and the monster came and stayed occasionally in the empty room linked to the house. I stood outside this house and looked all around in the neighborhood, wondering how fate has brought me back here decades after my childhood escapades to this house. I remembered the details about this house. I wanted to see inside and asked permission from the current residents. It was turned down, for, I understood, they thought, I was the original owner and had come back to take over the house! I was able to take a quick peek inside, as the lady turned back from the entry-door. Oh, my memories.

We returned to where the van was parked, so that we could drive back to Phillaur. At this time, Kundan Lal parted company, with our promise to stay in touch. We stayed in touch for the next several years, until his passing away in June 2007. Just like Manjeet, another very fine, gracious human being; I have missed him much.

4. Other Uncles' Houses

Just before we were ready to resume the return journey, I happened to mention another area of Jullundhur where close relatives lived—called "Chehar Bagh" ("Four-Gardens"). Jagjeet pointed his finger and said, "It is right there." We started walking in that direction. And there I found myself standing in front of the two-storied house of another uncle. I was allowed to peek inside. Then I recalled that the house of another uncle (now my father-in-law) was not far from here. We walked another block or so—and there it was, the birth-place of my wife. Memories flashed back; I remembered being in those houses during my childhood. What a day, indeed!

5. Daring Return Journey

Jagjeet parted company and I gratefully acknowledged his assistance. We were now ready to drive back to Phillaur. However, now another surprise; it was late evening and we found the front lights of the van were both burnt out! How do we get back? There were activities planned for the next day. The driver decided to follow a novel approach. He said he would slowly drive behind another vehicle, guided by the front lights of that vehicle! It seemed rather risky way of driving, one that would not be permitted about anywhere else in the world. I was quite apprehensive, yet I wanted to get back. Thankfully, we made it back in a couple of hours. Soon after, Rakesh Bharati came and informed me that if I wished, he would take me to the morning prayer-gathering next morning—Sunday, February 13th.

6. The Prayer Gathering

Visit to the prayer gathering was rather interesting—an open, tent-covered area. A large picture of the current Sikh guru (revered saint) was on display on an elevated block. As the devotees entered, they prostrated and touched and kissed the area in front of the picture, left some gifts, and then quietly sat down on the covered floor. A pious-looking woman was standing and delivering the sermon, with some other women sitting nearby, occasionally joining in the sermon. Pictures of Guru-Nanak and Jesus Christ were displayed on the adjacent wall. The sermon was about like I have often heard at the Unitarian-Fellowship gatherings—rather inclusive, mentioning the teachings of the Bible, the Qur'an, the Bhagwat-Geeta, the Garanth, and other sacred books, and often pointing to the One-Above (God, Allah, Bhagwan, etc.). Fascinating experience.

7. Ludhiana Wedding Reception

I had committed myself to join Chander Shekhar at the wedding reception in Ludhiana.

As instructed by him, I was taken there in a jeep, escorted

by two armed police guards and Rakesh Bharati—each of them quite relaxed with me. What was embarrassingly interesting was the experience of seeing the police guards occasionally getting out of the vehicle and clearing the traffic so we could move faster. As we reached the hotel, Chander came out to receive me, accompanied by several of his well-wishers, each showing much respect and obedience to him; after all, he was one of the rather influential police officials in the region. He introduced me as an honored guest. We walked inside for the reception, and he insisted that I should be next to him throughout; I obeyed.

8. Return to New Delhi

Later in the afternoon, I wished to get back to the Guest House and then return to Ludhiana for my journey back to New Delhi in the evening. Chander Shekhar was keen to bring me back in his new Mitsbushi Lancer. We did so, with the police jeep traveling behind—and again, the guards would get out occasionally to clear the way for the VIP car; it was embarrassing. I decided to ask Chander why this was necessary. He answered, "He enjoys being the big boss; it is his old habit."

We returned to my room and soon I was ready to go back to Ludhiana for my return journey to New Delhi. Chander Shekhar instructed Rakesh Bharati to accompany me, along with the driver and an armed police guard, to the Ludhiana railway station; his Mitsbushi Lancer was at our disposal for the journey. I gratefully said goodbye to him, with the understanding that we would stay in touch; and I gave one of my neckties to Chander Shekhar as a token of my appreciation for all the courtesies he extended to me. As I sat in the car, he made sure that, according to protocol, I alone sat in the back-seat, and the three escorts would sit separately in the front seat.

Uncomfortable as I was with the arrangement, after a few miles on the road, I asked Rakesh to sit along side me in the back-seat.

We arrived at the railway depot. And there I see my good friend, Manjeet Grewal, having specially come to say goodbye. Filled with sad emotions, we embraced each other again, with promises to stay in touch. He went out of my compartment and just before the train was ready to move, he returned for another goodbye embrace.

My four-day sentimental journey to the place of my origin began with a warm, emotional connection with Manjeet; and now it ended similarly at the moment of my departure from my roots. For so many reasons, we were unable to control our tears. Manjeet passed away in October 2001.

My friend received me at the New Delhi railway depot. In the next few days, I traveled to Aligarh where I was invited to give a lecture at the Aligarh University and then went to see one of the wonders of the world, the Taj Mahal, near Agra, India. Soon after, I flew back to the U.S.A., and after brief stopovers here and there, I returned home to my loving family.

My sacred pilgrimage was brief, but satisfying for my soul, so nostalgic, often agonizing and painful, yet comforting. There was the revival of old memories and the accumulation of new memories—always fresh and ever-lasting. Is there a closure? Perhaps not. Remembering my late father is easy; I do it every day. Missing him is the heartache that never goes away.

This narrative ends now. However, the pains and scar associated with memory never quite vanish. The saga of my odyssey will end only when my earthly sojourn ends.

EPILOGUE

This narrative is my story—my odyssey, based on memories and recollections of my childhood lived in the presence of a brutal step-father, the murderer of my own father. It is an account of my traumas, deprivations, desperations, struggles and survival. The memory of my late father has been most inspirational throughout my life, the source of what little I managed to accomplish in my life. Having survived in the bleakest of circumstances, I found "light at the end of the tunnel" in the land of opportunity; America is the only country where stories such as mine are still possible. And I am grateful for the trials—and opportunities—that led to my education and exposure to the world at large.

I recall a quote from late Albert Schweitzer (1875-1965), the eminent German philosopher and 1982 Nobel-Laureate: "In everyone's life, at some time, our inner fire goes out. It is then burst into flame by an encounter with another human being." In my case, the inner fire simmered down with the death of my father and then almost extinguished with the brutalities of a step-father. But, as I matured, the fire burst into a shining flame, always lit with the ever-present glow from the memory of my late father. Plus, I encountered so many sincere friends and mentors throughout my life who comforted and encouraged me with their kind words, supportive gestures, friendly smiles, and warmth of their handshakes; and I am ever so grateful.

And there is always the mercy of Almighty God, the most kind, the most benevolent.

APPENDIX

September 6, 1958—departure to USA

Dormitory living, 1960

*Summer Job 1960—Potlatch Lumber Mill
(Veneer Plant), Lewiston, Idaho*

Our shack, where I lived, 1960-62

Doctorated awarded 1968

Family picture, 1987

Economics and Enlightenment

GHAZI'S

"Try to leave the world a little better than the one you inherited. You'll never really know if you've succeeded – but have you tried?"

-S. M. Ghazanfar

BY NANCY GOULD-HILLIARD

Seeking peace and justice in a divided world actually does relate to supply and demand, free trade, public finance, global development and all the subjects taught in college economics.

At least that message has been transmitted over nearly four decades to more than 10,000 students of Shaikh Mohammed Ghazanfar, professor and chairman emeritus of economics at Idaho. Like the fabled shepherd who planted 100 acorns a day to transform French hillsides into oak forests, Ghazanfar advances human rights one lesson at a time – both in and out of the classroom.

An Indo-Pakistani refugee with Islamic roots, Ghazi, as he is widely known, has been part of the Palouse fabric for half a century. He considers himself a "citizen of the world" and Moscow, Idaho, his perch from which to view it. He is a voice of reason in times of crises and a wise mentor to students becoming world citizens.

Source: Here We have Idaho (University of Idaho Magazine), Fall 2007; pp.16-19

WORLD

Learning Moments

Andrianna Gurr '92, a counselor at Oregon Health and Science University, emulates Ghazi's "reaching out to those with multicultural values."

"During the first Gulf War, he helped us understand cultural differences and how not to generalize about people from Muslim countries. Ghazi made the economics of survival apparent to me. He blended the more mundane numbers with the human aspect of third-world economics. He inspired me to see the world beyond our very homogeneous campus."

Ghazi was born in India, and at age 10 his family was forced to migrate to Pakistan.

For Ghazi, history-making conflicts become "learning moments" to dispel stereotypical thinking about the Arab-Muslim culture and other prejudices. When the 2001 terrorist attack resulted in ethnic profiling and the jailing of an Idaho graduate student from Saudi Arabia, Ghazi emphasized the need to presume his innocence until proven guilty – regardless of appearances.

"As I drove home from campus (the evening of Sami Omar al-Hussayen's arrest in February 2002), I thought maybe there will be a bunch of police cars in front of my house," Ghazi was quoted in the Lewiston Morning Tribune. As a member of the Muslim faith, he said he felt vulnerable despite his 45 years of living here. "Fear has been rampant throughout the country, and now here."

As part of a Borah Symposium panel in 2005, Ghazi showed how propaganda shaped people's regard for most citizens of his background after 9-11.

He went further, in fact, said Idaho Rep. Tom Trail. "When international students were discriminated against, Ghazi stepped forward to work with everyone, writing and speaking about bringing people together to calm the situation."

Fulfilling his dream for a college education: Ghazi at Washington State University in 1960 from the Chinook yearbook.

The Prophet Mohammad did not base Islam on the sword, despite Western myth, Ghazi insists. "The name Islam signifies peace and reconciliation and is not violence-oriented. 'Jihad' means struggle to enhance personal and common welfare." Rather than generalize from the extremists, Ghazi urges better understanding of mainstream Islam.

Ghazi sees the brightest pathway via replacing polarized paranoia with pluralistic tolerance. Toward this end, he has written scholarly articles, presented papers at international meetings and documented historical truths.

One of Ghazi's students in the late 80s has become his colleague in the College of Business and Economics Steven Peterson, instructor and research economist, appreciates first hand Ghazi's 150 professional publications on public finance, economic development of third-world countries and Islamic contributions to the West.

"Ghazi mentored me all along the way, just as he has for others since the 1960s," says Peterson. "I now hear myself using his global perspective of the economic problems the planet faces. He has this disarming way of engaging people and stretching them to do their best. His passion is truly endearing."

Sidney Strong '02 is a lease accountant for Boeing aircraft. "Whenever I hear the word mentor, Ghazi comes to mind – so important to my academic and professional career. I'm sure I learned all about supply and demand from him, but Ghazi's encouragement left a lasting impression. He demanded the best from both good and struggling students. He taught me the importance of hard work, humility and determination."

Ghazi's Own Journey

Byron Dangerfield, former dean of the business college and Ghazi's boss for 16 years, says Ghazi lived "the great American success story, and that had a profound effect on students."

The road from Pakistan to Idaho molded Ghazi's compassion for the underdog. He came in 1958, as a 21-year-old with proof of admission to Washington State College, despite having only a 10th grade education and $50 to his name.

He soon became a homesick freshman at WSC who cried himself to sleep each night, and got up to a job scrubbing floors and doing dishes in order to survive.

"But when you are driven, you don't mind starving," he says, remembering this chance to help him escape the poverty and atrocities wrought by Partition in 1947, when the British left India divided in two. Pakistan had become the Islamic state and India a secular one.

Ghazi was just 10 when, and his family was forced to migrate from Philaur, India to Lahore, Pakistan with nothing but the clothes they were wearing. Energized by mob mentality, hundreds were crammed on buses, and his mother made him sit on the floor so as not to see all the carnage occurring outside the window.

In Lahore, they slept on the sidewalk until they could find shelter, and within months, his stepfather beseeched him to find foster homes, saying he could not afford to keep him. He shifted around, living with relatives, and when he matriculated 10th grade at age 14, he learned typing and shorthand. That became the modest means to survive and provide some kickback to his demanding stepfather. Further education had to be postponed, but the yearning never diminished.

When he began working for the U.S. Agency for International Development, he learned of opportunities to make a better life through more education, and WSC became his destination.

Once in Pullman in 1958, Ghazi struggled through his bachelor's degree work, knowing he had to maintain grades to keep his student visa, keep a job to send money home, pay his $50 rent, and live meagerly. He graduated with honors and was accepted into the master's program in economics. He felt as though he was on top of the world and even had a small stipend.

At age 28, with degrees in hand, he returned to Pakistan to visit his sisters and mother, and they introduced him to Rukhsana, his future wife. Just before they married in 1965, Ghazi cut off all ties with his bully stepfather and struck his final blow for freedom.

He and his new wife returned to the Palouse and Ghazi completed his doctorate in 1968 and began his teaching career at Idaho. He and Rukhsana set up housekeeping in Moscow where they established a family of three children and Rukhsana also earned a master's degree in counseling from Idaho.

Ghazi maintained international networks that enriched his teaching. During sabbaticals, he taught and researched at Punjab University in Pakistan and King Abdulaziz University in Saudi Arabia.

Today at 70, the semi-retired scholar and his wife "can't seem to get away from campus life and are so deeply embedded in the community, we can't move away from this wonderful place," he writes to a former student. The Ghazanfar's grown children, all educated at the University of Idaho, now live at three corners of the country.

Retirement, in Word Only

To refute the radical fringe image of the majority of Muslims, Ghazi recently published a compendium of 550 works in a book "Islamic Civilization: History, Contributions and Influence." It documents Arab-Islamic culture from 600 AD. The book is a window to literature pertaining to Islamic history and Islam's contributions to knowledge, and its influence in medieval Europe.

Ghazi's biggest challenge, he says, has been to connect intellectually and at the human level with others. His office hours are 24/7 and he has picked up foreign students at the airport or let them stay over until they get settled.

"I allow students to share their personal problems if they feel comfortable and let them know it's okay as long as they do their best. My advice to them is to give their adversaries a break. Don't hold grudges – learn to give. Recognize the positive outcomes of all associations."

Likewise he practices this approach as his own motivation. He dedicated his recent book to his father who died when Ghazi was 4. He "gave me so much in so little time. In a real sense, his death gave me life."

Ghazi's has won numerous distinguished faculty awards, community and humanitarian awards, and even a room in the J.A. Albertson Building is soon to be named Ghazi's Place Team Room. "It's a place where students can meet, discuss important issues of the day, and reflect on comments from their mentors, exactly the environment Professor Ghazanfar fostered during his many years of service to the University of Idaho," says Dean Jack Morris of College of Business and Economics.

Despite scores of recognitions, Ghazi's East-West nexus can trouble his psyche.

At times he has felt "the outsider" and even "the suspect." He once was interrogated by the FBI, making him wonder if the only acceptable Muslim is one who goes along with everything. It chilled his activism.

How best to strive for a new world order of common humanity? Ghazi urges individuals to "shuck arrogance and believe there's something to learn from everyone. Build bridges, avoid condescension or confrontation.

"Make it contagious." ∎

Pakistan Student To Reside In Yakima Valley For Summer

Quests for knowledge can lead men far, but few travel half the world to a foreign land to seek it. Ghazi Ghazanfar's quest has brought him from the capitol city in West Pakistan to a small agricultural community in the United States. His story is one of hard work and self discipline, but it is a story which has won for him the admiration and respect of many friends on this side of the ocean.

Ghazi's quest saw him to New York City by air in September of 1958. From there a long, tiring bus drive delivered him to his destination, Washington State University at Pullman. Following a year of academic pursuits, his wish for an American education brought him still further. At present, he is visiting in the Grandview community as a guest of Bruce Peterson, son of Mr. and Mrs. L. M. Peterson. He is employed for the summer months at the Peterson ranch. Crossing an ocean and two continents has brought him from his home in Karachi, West Pakistan, to the Yakima Valley, USA.

Ghazi, 22, nicknamed "Gus", is the only son in a family of six girls. His parents live in Hore, West Pakistan, where his stepfather is part owner in a textile mill. His deceased father was a high school teacher.

Before the partition of India in 1947, religious wars between the Moslems and Hindus cost the lives of millions. Ghazi, a Moslem, tells of his near escape from death at the hands of a clan of Hindus who were stopping all buses carrying Moslems. He said that such problems do not exist today since India has been divided into free countries.

Completes High School at 14

High school found Ghazi more interested in books than sports because of the age difference between him and his classmates. He had entered primary school at the age of five, but because his mother had already taught him the first two grades at home, Ghazi was promoted to the third grade on entry. By the time he was 14, he had already finished high school and was spending his time at a Pakistan university.

His command of the English language made available for him a job at the American Embassy, so he dropped out of college after 1½ years of study. In school Ghazi learned three languages starting with English at the age of eight. Other subjects included mathematics, health sciences, history and geographics.

American Embassy Assistant

Planning on four to six years at WSU, Ghazi will return to Pullman this fall as a sophomore majoring in business administration. While a resident of Karachi, he worked as an administrative assistant to the American Embassy. It was here that he chose his American college and field of study. Stationed at the Embassy is a foreign exchange board from WSU. Ghazi contacted them and after applying for a scholarship set out for New York with all tuition expenses paid for each year he attends the University. He must, however, finance his food and housing.

While at the State University, he has kept a 3.2 grade point average and is a member of the Cosmopolitan club. Recently he was nominated for the ASWSU International Relations Committee.

223

Faculty Profile — Shaikh Ghazanfar

Dr. Ghazanfar, who has been with the college for 25 years, says he has the "dubious distinction" of being the most senior faculty person.

"I am very fortunate," says Ghazi (his nickname since childhood), as he reflects on his life. Born in British India, he migrated to Pakistan at 10, when he was forced to leave home to live with relatives. He remembers yearning for education and walking to school barefoot. But when he graduated from high school at 14, he had to go to work to support his mother and sisters; higher education was a distant dream.

"Hard work paid off and after various jobs I ended up working at the American Embassy," says Ghazi. "At the Embassy were good friends who helped me get admitted to a U. S. university," (normally impossible without two years of college). Good luck and persistence resulted in acceptance at several universities, and WSU offered a tuition waiver. Thus, in 1958, at the age of 21, he landed in NYC with $50 in his pocket. "Just enough for a bus ticket to Pullman."

Dr. Shaikh Ghazan

"As a foreign student, you **must** make the grade. I scrubbed floors and cleaned pig pens and still sent money to my mother. I survived and graduated with honors," states Ghazi. He took a job at UI while completing his dissertation; then the college made him a good offer and he and his family decided to stay in the area. "I got many breaks in my life; now I wish to reciprocate."

Ghazanfar has seen many changes in the college in the past 25 years, including its departmentalization two years after he arrived. He notes the faculty "is much more research-oriented than it used to be," a trend he believes is positive. "You've got to produce—that's part of the job; that, in addition to fine leadership, is what got us accredited," he states.

> "I got many breaks in my life; now I wish to reciprocate."

He also has observed profound changes in the country's "social landscape" since 1958, "especially during the 70's," which he sees reflected in attitudes and behavior, and he says "I worry a lot about the future." Every available surface in Ghazanfar's office is covered with quotes and cartoons which he sees as "social commentary," and he sticks these "foods for thought" into exams, etc.

"My students are part of my extended family. If the day comes when I feel I'm not giving myself to my students, it's time to pack it in and retire. I'm sticky about performance and feel there are no free lunches," he claims.

> "My students are part of my extended family..."

Evidence of his work philosophy includes many years as part of a general-revenue forecast team for the Idaho legislature, numerous publications, and his acceptance this fall (for the second time) of the position as head of the economics department ("because somebody has to do it"). In addition, he received the Alumni Distinguished Faculty award in '83. He received the college's A. D. Davis award for distinguished service in '92, and he has received the Alumni Award for Excellence six times (the last being fall semester - 1993).

Dr. Ghazanfar rifled through numerous clippings to find a quote by Hillel that he feels sums up his views:

> "If I am not for myself, who will be for me?
> And if I am for mine own self, what am I?"

Enterprise

College of Business and Economics

University of Idaho

Spring 1994

Economics professor "Ghazi" Ghazanfar is grateful that WSU gave him his start.

Ghazanfar finds his
'land of
opportunity'

sisters. He learned typing and shorthand, skills
that helped land him a clerical job in 1955, the
U.S. Agency for International Development hired
him at the U.S. Embassy in Karachi, Pakistan.

"All along I had this intense yearning for
learning," he said.

Friends and superiors at the USAID wrote to a
handful of U.S. universities on Ghazanfar's behalf, asking that he be admitted despite only 10
years of schooling. The letter touted his fluency
in English, work ethic and maturity. WSU had an
exchange program with Pakistan at the time. He
was admitted as a freshman and WSU gave him a
tuition scholarship amounting to $400.

"Those were big bucks then," the economist
says.

With the money he had saved, he purchased a
one-way plane ticket to New York, rode a bus
across the country, and arrived in Pullman on
Sept. 14, 1958 with $50 in his pocket. Soon he

Source: _Hilltopics_ (Washington State
University Magazine), June 2000

COMMENTARY

11/16/07

WSU alumni award goes to Ghazanfar

The Washington State University Alumni Achievement Award, created in 1970, is the school's highest alumnus award. It recognizes and honors alumni who have given outstanding service. Selected individuals are those who have rendered "significant service to WSU and/or outstanding contributions to community and/or profession and/ or nation. Out of an estimated 250,000 graduates, only 465 have received this prestigious award.

Last month, the INKster's old friend S. M. "Ghazi" Ghazanfar became the 466th person to receive this honor. Ghazi, who lives in Moscow, is professor emeritus of economics at the University of Idaho and was director of the International Studies Program there from 1989 to 1993.

"I was truly blessed," Ghazi noted in an e-mail to the INKster last week. "Some of my key WSU mentors and some professional peers from around the nation had nominated me and to my good fortune, I was selected."

The award ceremony took place Oct. 6. In addition to Ghazi's immediate family, the gathering included friends from across the country and "numerous" WSU faculty, staff and students. WSU Provost/Executive Vice President Robert Bates presented the award.

Vera White

INK

And on Oct. 27, Ghazi and other Alumni Achievement Award recipients were inducted into the WSU "Wall of Honor," an event organized by WSU's College of Agricultural, Human and Natural Resource Sciences.

"That is the college in which economics, my field, is now located," Ghazi explained. "After the ceremony, the recipients were all guided to the 'Wall of Honor' (on the fourth floor of Hulbert Hall) where our pictures were hung."

The INKster finds it nearly impossible when referencing Ghazi not to add that he is, without doubt, one of the finest gentlemen she has ever had the pleasure to know.

226

ALUMNI
ACHIEVEMENT
AWARD

Dr. Shaikh M. Ghazanfar '62, '64 & '69

For outstanding contributions to the understanding of Islamic studies and culture, especially relating to economics, and for being an advocate of higher education as teacher, presenter and author enriching the lives of many students both at the University of Idaho and Washington State University.

GIVEN IN PULLMAN, WASHINGTON,

THIS SIXTH DAY OF OCTOBER,

TWO THOUSAND AND SEVEN

ALUMNI ASSOCIATION PRESIDENT

EXECUTIVE DIRECTOR

WASHINGTON STATE UNIVERSITY
ALUMNI ASSOCIATION

Jack Morris, S. M. Ghazanfar and Dean Byron Dangerfield celebrate friendship and Ghazi's retirement.

Can it be? Ghazi retiring?

After 34 years of distinguished service to the University of Idaho and the College of Business and Economics, S. M. "Ghazi" Ghazanfar retired last May. He couldn't bid farewell to the CBE and its students just yet, however; he is teaching on a part-time basis during the 2002-2003 academic year.

Throughout his tenure, Ghazanfar demonstrated a balanced commitment to teaching, research and service. His involvement with students and his desire to see that they were well educated and successful are legendary. He still receives e-mails and letters from former students, updating him on their professional and personal lives. He responds to each one.

The thought of retirement was difficult for Ghazanfar. As he has stated numerous times, "This university and my former students have made me what I am today; they are my life." This was not meant as a derogatory slant against his wife of 37 years, Rukshana, or his three children, whom he loves dearly. Talking about his children and two grandsons brings a smile to his face. However, his "extended family," as he calls his students, present and past, have remained a top priority for Ghazanfar. One of the CBE's recent graduates reflects upon her former professor as a "truly self-made man who embodies excellence as a teacher, as a learner, and also as a human being."

Professor Ghazanfar has received numerous faculty achievement awards including 15 Alumni Excellence Awards, the UI Distinguished Faculty Award, Panhellanic Faculty of the year Award, ASUI Outstanding Faculty Award, as well as the CBE's A.D. Davis Faculty Fellow on two separate occasions. His research record also is most impressive: almost 50 national and international journal publications, two books, and approximately 150 conference papers and presentations.

When asked if he plans on staying in Moscow, Ghazanfar will only say, "Rukshana and I haven't decided yet. Moscow and Pullman have been my home for 45 years since I received my degrees from Washington State University. How can I leave what I know so well and love so much?" He admits that his daughter, who lives in the Atlanta area, pulls at his heartstrings when she gives him a few "subtle" nudges about moving there so his "grandsons will know their grandfather." However, Ghazanfar, being ever so cautious, thinks he needs more time to contemplate a move.

He recently signed another book contract and feels the resources at UI are invaluable to him, so no move will be made before the end of the year. "After I have completed my book, we shall see," he said with the usual shrug and hand in the air. Typical Ghazi expression.

UI/CBE, Enterprise, Spring 2003

Retirement, Ghazanfar Style

By Diane Lugar

For a man who has enjoyed teaching over half of his life, retirement doesn't come easily, nor does it mean giving up what has been such an important part of his existence. Although S. M. "Ghazi" Ghazanfar officially retired from the University of Idaho in 2002, he has returned to the College of Business and Economics as an adjunct professor to teach economics, continue his research, publish articles and books and establish new relationships with students. Teaching and the camaraderie with the young men and women he encountered have shaped this man.

Ghazanfar recently wrote the following to one of his former students. "During all of my 36+ years at Idaho, I have been most fortunate to have encountered many, many young folks who have inspired me in becoming a better mentor, teacher, friend and, above all, a better human being. And in the process, I tried to convey to my young friends—with all the TLC I could muster—things meaningful not only in earning a living but also in living a life. I am personally so much better off for all of that. And there is no conceivable way to tangibly measure the worth of all those connections. They touch the soul; they nurture the spirit; and they give meaning to life; and there is no substitute, none whatsoever."

The impact he made was reciprocated by many of his former students including Jeff Stoddard, '75, Accounting, who recently made a second substantial gift to the CBE building campaign. With his latest donation, he honored one of his favorite professors by naming the Ghazanfar Team Room in the student level of the J. A. Albertson Building. Stoddard explained his reason for the gift—"I am very appreciative of the knowledge and experiences that I gained at the University of Idaho and the wonderful professors and classmates that I got to learn from. It is my pleasure to help the University when I can. I also am happy to help honor one of the University's finest educators."

The city of Moscow, Idaho, also honored Ghazanfar with the first biennial Community Unity Award this past year for his decades of work by actively promoting diversity and human rights. According to Ghazanfar, "it's not self glorification. You just try to do what you think is right." In his over 48 years in the area, as a WSU student and then on the Idaho faculty, he has been involved with the Latah County Human Rights Task Force, helped to initiate activities celebrating Martin Luther King's birthday and a forthcoming CommUNITY Walk. He also participated in civil rights activities in the 1960s. He currently serves as a member of the Moscow Human Rights Commission.

In addition to his teaching and civic duties, Ghazanfar finds the time to continue his research. Earlier this year, his 558-page book, "Islamic Civilization: History, Contributions, and Influence: A Compendium of Literature," was released. The book addresses the connections between early Islam and the Latin-West which he says "are inextricably linked together in terms of the sources of enlightenment, renaissance, reformation and even the beginning of the 17th century modern science, with the Greeks in the background." Last April, he presented a University of Idaho interdisciplinary-colloquium seminar on a topic related to that book. Also, over the years he has published several student-generated research papers, the most recent, with Tyson Rallens, '06, entitled, "Microfinance: Recent Experience, Future Possibilities, Journal of Social, Political and Economic Studies, Summer 2006.

For a man who is "officially" retired, it doesn't appear that Ghazanfar has quit pursuing his passions—teaching, writing and touching the hearts of those around him. ⊕

UI/CBE, Enterprise, Spring 2007

229

FRIDAY,
MAY 10, 2002

Reception at the UI to honor Ghazanfar

Shaikh M. Ghazanfar, lovingly known as "Ghazi," is hanging it up after 34 years as professor of economics at the University of Idaho.

A reception in his honor is planned from 3 to 5 p.m. Wednesday at the UI Commons Aurora Room.

In a prepared release, Nancy Hilliard, UI spokeswoman, posed the question: "Now how can this man, who first came to this area in 1958 to earn a degree at Washington State University, leave now — with lessons still for us to learn?"

The INKster, along with all who know this respected educator, appreciates Hilliard's concern — especially in these troubled times.

**VERA
WHITE**

INK

See INK, Page 8A

INK

from page 1A

ciates Hilliard's concern — especially in these troubled times.

Having been through war in his homeland of pre-partitioned India, he migrated to Pakistan in 1947. He earned his bachelor's, master's and doctorate degrees from WSU. After joining the faculty at the UI, he served as chairman of the economics department, was a 15-time winner of the Alumni Award for Faculty Excellence, won the UI Outstanding Faculty Award ASUI in 1994 and other honors too numerous to list.

In addition to conducting dozens of research projects and authoring several books, Ghazi has been the resident expert on the Palouse in early Islam culture and its contributions to society. He contributed to the PBS Series "Islam: Empire of Faith" (1999-2001).

According to Ghazi's predictions, the higher education of tomorrow will be more interdisciplinary, global and learner-oriented.

"Our nation must become better at listening and dialoging with other nations," said Ghazi, a man aptly described by Hilliard as a "philosopher with an applied bent whose passions punctuate his teachings."

We hope Ghazi doesn't stray too far from the Palouse when he retires. We need him now as never before.

MOSCOW CommUNITY WALK
PROCLAMATION & DEDICATION

WHEREAS, 2013 marks the 7th consecutive year of Moscow's CommUNITY Walk, the vision of longtime human rights advocate S.M. 'Ghazi' Ghazanfar; and

WHEREAS, This event celebrates and nourishes Moscow's reputation as a welcoming, inclusive community; and

WHEREAS, Moscow Human Rights Commission; Latah County Human Rights Task Force; the Office of Human Rights, Access, and Inclusion at the University of Idaho; the Northwest Coalition for Human Rights; the City; University; and our many allies are committed protecting civil and human rights through social justice and unity; and

WHEREAS, Human rights are advanced by through relationships, policies, and practices that support equality and fairness for all people; and

WHEREAS, Moscow's CommUNITY Walk symbolizes our commitment to preserving and enhancing peace and understanding among individuals from all backgrounds and persuasions; and

WHEREAS, In 2007, CommUNITY Walk founder S.M. 'Ghazi' Ghazanfar described the inaugural event as "...simply a walk. We're walking together;" and

WHEREAS, Our fondly-regarded 'Ghazi' and Rukhsana will be missed when they move to Atlanta this spring;

NOW, THEREFORE, I, Nancy Chaney, Mayor for the City of Moscow, do hereby proclaim Saturday, April 27th, 2013 as

CommUNITY Walk Day

In the City of Moscow, and extend special recognition to the Ghazanfars, who exemplify the ideals of unity and inclusivity, and who have given so much of themselves to our community over these many years, and I urge everyone to participate in this year's event as they are able, and to promote compassionate connections throughout our community, region, and world.

DATED this 27th day of April, 2013

Nancy J. Chaney, Mayor

Shaikh Ghazanfar, or "Ghazi," has been at the University of Idaho for 31 years and is head of the US economics department.

Anne Drobish
Daily News

Immigrants face travails

Daily News, Monday, July 12, 1999

UI professor recalls boyhood fears, adult taunts

The journey was 90 miles, but it seemed like 900 to a 10-year-old boy.

The date was maybe Aug. 29 or 30, 1947 (he isn't sure of the exact date).

Shaikh M. Ghazanfar, known as "Ghazi," boarded one of the buses with family, friends and neighbors from the small town of Philaur, East Punjab, in what was then British India. Around them, a small military convoy in Jeeps provided minimal protection for those seeking refuge in a divided country

where "friends were no longer friends."

"Everything was left behind because people were more important than things," said Ghazanfar, recalling those dark days in 1947. "I guess there also was this feeling that we will come back."

The old buses crept along. Dead bodies littered the roadside, some floating in a nearby river.

"My mother would often push my head down," he said.

His most vivid memory is of a man standing on the foot board

area holding a bar for balance.

"I still get goose bumps when I talk about it today," he said last week, interrupting his story.

The man was standing there like all the others who crammed in the bus and eagerly awaited crossing the border into Pakistan.

All of a sudden, someone from outside the bus attacked the man with a sword. Blood streamed from a large gash on his arm, but he did not let go of the bar.

See Ghazanfar back page

TINA McCLURE

PALOUSE PEOPLE

MOSCOW-PULLMAN DAILY NEWS
(Monday July 12 1999)

Ghazanfar

from page 1A

TINA McCLURE

PALOUSE PEOPLE

Even today, Ghazanfar — a professor and head of the department of economics at the University of Idaho — can't help but ask what if.

"What if the bus had stopped for the injured man?"

"What if he had fallen?"

"What might be the next phase?"

But the buses eventually reached Pakistan.

His family slept on the sidewalks for several days until they found shelter.

There was little money for his family to survive and Ghazanfar's stepfather could no longer care for him.

"My mother was helpless, but said somehow I must get an education."

Ghazanfar was shuffled between relatives until he graduated from high school at age 14.

With no support for college, he went to work. He learned to type and take shorthand.

After various jobs, he was hired in 1956 at the U.S. Embassy in Pakistan with the Agency for International Development.

Ghazanfar wanted more.

"One of the most strong driving forces for me is to think of my father and what he would like me to accomplish," he said.

Ghazanfar's father, a high school teacher, died when he was 2. He doesn't remember his father and any pictures were left behind the day his family fled in 1947.

Because Ghazanfar only had a high school education, admission to a U.S. college was a long shot. However, with help from from U.S. Embassy friends, he was accepted to three schools and chose Washington State University which gave him a tuition waiver. He arrived in New York on Sept. 6, 1958, and took a bus to Pullman.

Ghazanfar worked his way through school washing floors, dishes and large pans in the dining hall.

"There were times when there was only one meal a day," he said. "But when you are driven by a goal you don't mind doing some of these things."

He also worked summers at the Potlatch Mill and picked fruit in Yakima so, he could send

money to his family in Pakistan.

He received his bachelor's degree in business administration and a master's degree in economics.

In 1965, he visited Pakistan to marry Rukhsana Sharif. The couple returned to Pullman where Ghazanfar completed his doctoral degree in economics.

He and his wife have raised three children in Moscow: Farah, 31; Asif, 27, and Kashif, 23. He has one grandson, Rafay, 9.

"It's been wonderful in so many ways," he said. "I have so much to be thankful for in the way of opportunities."

And yet, there have been hard times. There have been unkind words and stares, even after 41 years in the United States and 31 years at the UI.

"When you are, The Other you are always 'The Other,'" he said, writing the words in the middle of a single sheet of white notebook paper. "That kind of assimilation is not possible, especially when you look different and talk a little different. Sometimes, I think I expect too much of other human beings."

He said he always felt a little uneasy as a student, and when he and his family moved into their home on F Street in Moscow, they had problems with barking dogs and rude neigh-

bors. He will not forget the names he was called, such as "camel jockey" and "sand nigger."

Then there is the subtle racism. The feeling he has that he must work twice as hard to get credit and constantly prove himself.

"It makes you wonder, are you just being tolerated or being accepted," he said.

And it's not just in the past. Less than a year ago, some anti-Muslim and anti-Arab propaganda was posted on the bulletin board outside his UI office.

Yet, Ghazanfar said he tries to rise above it.

He said the answer is not clear. Education, sensitivity training and awareness all will promote a better understanding of one another. A community forum on diversity might help, he said.

"There are so many things that are wonderful, you have to take the bad with the good. Some things in life you accept. You hope they change, but if they don't, you just accept it."

Tina McClure is city editor at the Daily News. Her column Palouse People *runs on Mondays. She can be reached at (208) 882-5561, ext. 233 or at <editor@moscow.com>.*

232

Source: <u>Legendary Locals of Moscow, Idaho</u>; Latah Count Historical Society, published by Arcadia Publishing, Charleston, South Carolina; 2015; p.82

Shaikh "Ghazi" Ghazanfar
One of two recipients of the Sheikh Community Unity Award in 2005 was retired professor Shaikh "Ghazi" Ghazanfar. Ghazi's childhood in British India was tainted by ethnic violence, which spurred him to join the US Civil Rights movement of the 1960s. In Moscow, he advocated for human rights both on and off campus. He organized the town's now annual CommUNITY Walk and was a founding member of the Human Rights Commission.

Professor Ghazanfar contributes to PBS series

Fondly known to most as "Ghazi", Chairman of the Department of Economics, Professor S. Ghazanfar is a contributing scholar to a documentary being produced for the Public Broadcasting Service (PBS). The three part series is tentatively titled, "West and the Islamic Civilization." Ghazanfar is one of 17 international scholars contributing material for the documentary, and he also is assisting in editing the script for approval.

Ghazanfar has explored and written extensively on the contributions of Islamic scholastics in the field of economics during the Golden Age of Islam, from 700 to 1400 A.D. Most recently, his research has explored the evolution of medieval social thought generally among Islamic scholastics and linkages with Latin-Europe.

From the 7th to the 13th century, the Islamic civilization was at its peak, stretching from Spain and North Africa to India and beyond. At the same time, Europe was experiencing its Dark Ages, a period many scholars consider the "great gap" in world-wide human intellectual evolution. Ghazanfar contends those scholars limit their vision to Europe and disregard

intellectual activity in the rest of the world.

"They ignore the fact that this was the period when Islamic civilization, building on the rediscovered Greek heritage, contributed enormously to knowledge in all its dimensions – there was massive transfer of that knowledge to Europe through translations, travels, cultural diffusion and the Crusades," said Ghazanfar.

He describes the Islamic Golden Age as a giant melting pot, marked by pluralism, tolerance and acceptance of people of all faiths. The Islamic faith not only encouraged the pursuit of ideas and knowledge, it was a religious duty. In terms of economics, Ghazanfar said medieval Islamic scholastics developed numerous economic concepts and ideas that are remarkably similar to those found in contemporary books – voluntary exchange, right to private property incentives, profit maximization, division of labor and specialization, the role of agriculture and trade and public finance issues. He describes the Islamic economy as a capitalistic economy, but one with a heart offering concern for the welfare of the masses. Ghazanfar compares it to the

"mixed-capitalism" U. S. economy where an emphasis on private enterprise is balanced with governmental spending on social issues.

Ghazanfar, who has been with the UI since 1968, calls himself Western by training and outlook, but with Islamic heritage. Originally migrating from Pakistan in 1958, he received all his post-secondary education in the U. S. At the UI he has earned numerous honors, including 10 Alumni Awards for Faculty Excellence.

Ghazanfar said the script for the PBS documentary is currently in the process of gaining final approval from contributing scholars and the program will likely be produced at the end of this year or the beginning of next year.

[Reprinted from the University of Idaho Register, *September 11, 1998]*

DESH SEWAK, Chandigarh, India; Sunday, February 27, 2000
(Daily Newspaper)

A MEETING WITH DR. GHAZANFAR, A CITIZEN OF THE WORLD

Born in Phillaur, went to Pakistan during independence, now a citizen of America,
Dr. S.M. Ghazanfar said that India and Pakistan spend a lot on defence—and that is a reason that,
inspite of having resources, there is little development/progress here.

Dr. Ghazanfar's father, S.M. Bakhsh, was a teacher in Government Senior Secondary School
here. He died in March 1941 and Dr. Ghazanfar was only 4 years old at the time. Now Dr.
Ghazanfar came here because of the contact with school's principal, Shri Prem Kumar, and by
visiting his birthplace and father's school, he could not stop his tears. Memories of childhood, the
home where he spent 10 years of his life, the streets where he played, he felt like going to these
places again. I met Dr. Ghazanfar in school where he was gaining knowledge about the school
from Shri Prem Kumar. Dr. Ghazanfar is now a Professor and Chairman, Department of
Economics in a University in America. Dr. Ghazanfar told that after the death of his father, his
mother married again. He had a tough time living with his step-father. During independence he
and the family migrated to Pakistan. He continued his education in difficult times. After 10th
class he started doing a job by learning typing and shorthand. Somehow he managed to go to the
USA. After doing bachelor's degree and M.Sc. In 1962 in America, he did his Ph.D. in 1968.
Before marriage, he suffered lot of atrocities from his step-father.

Talking about Pakistan-Hindustan, Dr. Ghazanfar said the culture of the people is similar. People
are emotional here. While teaching in the University, the students here are like a family, but
students in the U.S, are like adopted. While talking to him, he being a professor in economics
said that both of these nations have a lot of poverty. If the stomach is empty, then what do we give
independence? We have a lot of manpower here which is not being used effectively.

After visiting his birthplace, he presented a seminar at the Aligarh University and then made a
presentation at the Society of the History and Economic Thought in a seminar in Austria. Calling
himself the citizen of the world, Dr. Ghazanfar left Phillaur with memories of his birthplace and
his father.

Sarabjeet Gill

(Exact translation of the article published in Gurmakhi language)

(handwritten, left margin) SENTIMENTAL JOURNEY TO MY ROOTS, FEB 2000

ਦੇਸ਼ ਸੇਵਕ, ਚੰਡੀਗੜ੍ਹ, ਐਤਵਾਰ 27 ਫਰਵਰੀ, 2000

ਦੁਨੀਆਂ ਦਾ ਨਾਗਰਿਕ ਅਖਵਾਉਣ ਵਾਲੇ ਡਾ. ਗਜ਼ਾਨਫਰ ਨਾਲ ਇਕ ਮੁਲਾਕਾਤ

Printed in the United States
By Bookmasters